READING TUTOR

READING TUTOR

HOW TO HELP YOUR FIRST OR SECOND GRADER BECOME GREAT AT READING

Mary Kay Linge

NEW YORK

Copyright © 2000 LearningExpress, LLC.

Library of Congress Cataloging-in-Publication Data:

Linge, Mary Kay.
    Reading tutor / by Mary Kay Linge.
        p. cm.
    ISBN 1-57685-340-3
    1. Reading (Primary) 2. Reading—Parent participation.
   3. Tutors and tutoring. I. Title.

LB1525 .L66 2000
                            00-056299

Printed in the United States of America

9 8 7 6 5 4 3 2 1

First Edition

For more information or to place an order, contact LearningExpress at:

900 Broadway
Suite 604
New York, NY 10003

Or visit us at:

www.learnatest.com

Contents

Acknowledgments

▼

The assistance of an advisory board of teachers and parents made this book possible, and I thank them deeply for their help. Laurie Chambers of the Marion Street School in Lynbrook, New York; Donna Cook of the Ilene T. Feldkirchner School in Green Brook, New Jersey; and Susan Todd of Our Lady of Good Counsel School in Staten Island, New York generously shared their time, materials, and expertise. Patti Gallo of Dover, Delaware; Venise Mulé-Glass of Commack, New York; and Liz Townsend of Alexandria, Virginia opened their homes and hearts to me in the hope that their experiences would be useful to fellow parents. In addition, recognition goes to teachers Maureen Murray, Tina M. Roberts, and Katie R. Barry who contributed ideas for some of the lesson plans you will find in Chapter 5.

I'm grateful for the thoughtful critiques and insights of many other educators and parents, particularly Frances Santangelo, Debbie Rizzoli, Cathy O'Brien, Suzanne Crew, and Diane Ohe. My exuberant children, Magdalene, Peter, and Teresa, served as (mostly) willing guinea pigs for the fun and games of Chapter 6 and for many other recommendations throughout the book. And, as ever, I'm indebted to my husband Tom Wrobleski, whose patient coaching has gotten me through some of the toughest challenges of my life, this one included.

But most of all I'm grateful to Mary Linge, my first teacher. Now that she's gone professional, I'm as proud of her as she's always been of me. Thanks, Mom.

READING TUTOR

▼

1

What Every Parent Needs to Know about Reading

▼

In the first and second grades, the most important educational goal is to help students become comfortable with *words*—wherever they encounter them—through writing, listening, working with letters, and reading, reading, reading. By now your child's teacher has undoubtedly stressed how important it is for you to stay involved with your child's education, especially where reading is concerned. But in the context of your daily life and your child's everyday experience, what does "involvement" really mean? This book will outline the most effective and efficient ways to help your child become a great reader; from knowing your child's learning style, to understanding what is going on in their classroom, to giving you practical ideas about what you can do to help your child.

DISCOVERING YOUR CHILD'S LEARNING STYLE

As a parent, you have unique insights into your child. After all, you have seen her at her best and worst moments: when she's tired and when she's alert, when she's happy and when she's upset. You know what interests her, what motivates her, and how she thinks. The beauty of all this critical information is that you can actually use it to help her learn in the way that is best for her. It's important to keep in mind that there is no one "right" way to read—just as there is no single manner in which to teach reading and language arts. Sometimes, a difference in teaching style can make all the difference. Your child who's been struggling for half of first grade will suddenly "get it" when given a different approach to reading.

How We Learn

Educators speak of intelligence in many ways, but one of the more popular concepts in recent years is that of multiple intelligences. The idea is that there are many ways to learn, and that students can best be reached and taught through their own particular learning style. While many classification systems have been described, one way to understand learning styles is by linking them to the various senses.

Auditory learners are most successful when they can use the sense of hearing. If your child can follow complex spoken instructions, easily memorizes songs and nursery rhymes, and can comprehend a story that is read to him even without the help of pictures to follow, he may be an auditory learner.

Kinesthetic learners need to incorporate movement into the intellectual process. The kinesthetic learner doesn't simply have a high energy level (although she may); she'll just have an easier time understanding a new idea if she can associate it with action. If your child gesticulates as she talks, paces while she thinks, acts out stories as she tells them, or seems to understand how to do something only after she has actually performed the action, she may have a kinesthetic tendency.

Tactile learners rely on the sense of touch as a prime learning tool. Physical form means a lot to them, and they learn best when they can associate a new idea with something they've actually felt or held. If your child learned his shapes by handling building blocks and his letters by working an alphabet puzzle, he may respond to tactile teaching techniques.

Visual learners do best when they can see new ideas in writing, on video, or in some physical shape. They are highly conscious of color and light in their surroundings. A child who can retell a movie's plot line after one viewing, insists on following the words as you read to her, and makes a point of committing ideas to paper in writing or drawing may be a visual learner. (To help your child learn to read in the way that is best for him, see Chapter 3 for tips and information about how to observe your child in a way that will help you support his particular learning style.)

Knowing that every classroom contains students with every learning style, good teachers strive to shape their lessons so that the needs of everyone in the class will be met. Many use the five senses as a planning template. If a decoding skill is being taught, for example, children are instructed to listen to the sound of a letter as they look at the written letter, so that they can both see and hear it. Then the children make the sound of the letter with their mouths and write the sound using their hands. Finally, children are encouraged to get up on their feet and write the letter out on the board.

If you know your child's learning strengths and weaknesses, you can help him prepare to be optimally receptive to new concepts—in short, you can set him up for success. For example, visual learners have a hard time remembering things they haven't seen, so spoken instructions at home or on a test can leave them completely lost. Therefore, encourage your visual learner to take notes. Write chores on a chart so that he will remember them; ask his teacher to remind him to write down homework instructions.

In traditional classroom settings, where instruction is geared toward visual and auditory reinforcement, kinesthetic and tactile learners can run into trouble. If this is your child's learning orientation, discuss the matter with your child's teacher early on. In all likelihood he will have good suggestions to help you assist your child with lessons at home. For example, hands-on games such as Dough Letters and Flash Card Charades are an excellent means of teaching kinesthetic and tactile learners how to read. (See Chapter 6 for more information about these games.) In order to make traditional lessons more meaningful, and to encourage him to listen and observe in a fun way, you may also want to help your child practice his listening and visual skills with games such as I Spy and Riddle Me This (also described in Chapter 6).

BEING PROACTIVE IN YOUR CHILD'S EDUCATION

Almost any teacher will tell you that you have a special advantage as a parent—*you* are the one who really knows your child's ins and outs, her idiosyncrasies, and the things that make her feel most comfortable. No matter how astute or observant the teacher, he sees your child only for a limited amount of time each day, which makes your role in her education all the more important. Knowing what you already know, you can work with her and her teacher to reinforce school lessons at home.

Being proactive runs the gamut from simple yet specific discussions with your child ("So, what was your reading story about today?") to elaborate action plans that you and the teacher construct together. A wealth of learning material—board games, videos, flash cards, web sites, CD-ROMs, workbooks, tutoring programs, etc.—is available to help you support your child's reading program. Choosing among all these products can feel like an overwhelming task, but Chapter 9 takes a clear-eyed look at the options. Some parents get involved with their children's education by volunteering to be a class parent, a designated reader, or a lunchroom helper. They find that even a limited presence in school has a positive effect on their children. For them it's important to do something active that shows their children that they're "there" and that they care. Some children simply need to see that you know their school and want to hear you say, "Hey, I walked down your hallway today" or "I saw your picture hanging up." This involvement shows a child that his education matters to you. Many teachers strive to offer working parents opportunities to become involved in the classroom in ways that will fit into their challenging schedules. For example, one second-grade teacher asks parents to volunteer to tape-record themselves reading her chosen "book of the week." The children listen to the tapes in class and follow along with the reading. Their parents love being able to "read" to the class even if they can't be there in person. Some give particularly creative, dramatic readings, which inspire the children to try to guess whose parent it is. Ask your child's teacher if there are any ways you can pitch in, no matter what your schedule is.

There may be a time, however, when your role as a parent will be to take the lead in discerning, evaluating, and correcting a learning problem. Don't assume that your child's teacher is the only person who is qualified to detect and deal with an academic problem. It's a good idea to keep tabs on your child's learning progress, even in a very simple way. For example, if she seems to be "stuck" in her reading—if for two or three months she still struggles with the same words or ideas—you may need to ask her classroom teacher for help in investigating further.

Proactiveness doesn't have to cost anything more than your time and attention—two of the most important gifts you can give your child as she works on becoming a great reader.

WHAT YOU NEED TO KNOW

If you're ready to help your child become a successful reader there are some practical things you do need to know about the process itself.

Teaching Methods

In the past several years, two divergent approaches to literacy learning—*phonics* and the *whole-language* method—have been used to train young readers. In brief, the phonics method focuses on "sounding out" words from the letters that comprise them; the whole-language method trains students to recognize complete words.

Most educators today blend the best elements of both approaches into a system that encourages children to use phonics *and* whole language to tackle unfamiliar material. Still, it's important for parents to understand the basics of both systems, as well as the philosophy that's actually in use in your child's classroom. A reading problem may stem from the method being used to teach him. (Please see Chapter 2 for an in-depth discussion of various learning methods.)

How Do Children Become Good Readers?

The answer is straightforward. Good readers read a lot. They read for enjoyment as well as for information, and they don't often need to be prompted to pick up a book, newspaper, or magazine.

Good readers also tend to see others reading with frequency and pleasure. If the adults in a child's life don't make a habit of reading themselves, the child will see little reason to do so. Your assignment, then, is to let your child see you reading this book, as well as a novel, a magazine, and your local paper. Your own enjoyment of reading will quietly inspire your child to become a reader, too.

In some households the arrival of the morning newspaper is an important event: The weather, local, comics, and style pages are quickly divvied up between children and adults. In other families books are a real presence throughout the house—many on low shelves so that the children can reach them easily. Knowing where all the Dr. Seuss books are, and helping Mom or Dad to put them away, and in order, gives children the message that reading is an integral part of life. Finally, it's important to talk about what you've read, at the dinner table or in the car, or at bath time. Some parents have noted that the most interesting family discussions revolve around books—just by asking a question as basic as "Did you get it?" The idea isn't necessarily to launch a formal family book group, although you might try it (see Chapter 6 for ideas), but to plant the notion that there *is* something important to be gained from reading after all.

BECOMING READING PARTNERS

Your good example will set the stage, but it's only a beginning. Reading together is a huge factor in helping your child develop into a great reader. According to Laurie Chambers, a reading specialist, "it's important not only to read with your child every night; you need to *listen* to him read every night and ask questions such as, 'what did you like about the story? Why did you like this part?' These literal questions guide young readers back into the story to find the answers."

When Parents Read to Children

Reading aloud to your children shouldn't end when you pack up the board books. Many families continue to read bedtime stories long after their children have outgrown *Goodnight Moon*, and choose books that are well beyond their classroom reading levels. Some lists include the *Harry Potter* series; James Herriott's pet stories, such as *All Creatures Great and Small*; the *Little House* series; the *Ramona* books by Beverly Cleary; or a timeless classic, like *Charlotte's Web*. No matter how old they are, children still enjoy being read to and will often ask questions about a story or words they don't understand. This is a great opportunity for a child to soak up new information or develop an appreciation for the intricacies of plot and character development. A book sometimes has the power to really grab a young reader, so that he'll want to explore more books by the same author or in the same genre. For some children, picture books may provide visual images that are counter-productive to improving reading skills. Under these circumstances, it might be better to keep the illustrations out of her view, when you're sharing a book. Instead, let her visualize the action using her imagination. You can stop reading at appropriate intervals to check on her overall comprehension of the story and her understanding of important details.

Reading sessions go more smoothly if you're prepared. If it's possible, read a book all the way through, before reading it out loud, or choose a book you remember well from your own childhood.

Before you begin a new book, judge it by its cover. Talk about the title with your child, examine the jacket or cover art, and read the flaps or the back-panel copy together. Try to predict what the story will be about. (See Chapter 6 for making prediction a game.)

A little drama never hurts. Get into the spirit of the story with different voices for various characters; use simple sound effects like whistling, clapping, finger-snapping, and so on; and as much excitement as you can muster. But always be sure to use your voice in "reading" punctuation marks. Model the way sentences should be read by pausing at commas, raising your pitch for question marks, stopping at periods, and so on.

When Children Read to Parents

When you are reading aloud from a book that is at your child's reading level, try alternating pages—you read one page, your child reads the next. This way she can hear the differences between the way you read and the way she reads. An important benefit of reading together is that it helps your child learn to associate the rhythms of speech with the conventions of the written word. If your child ignores punctuation signals as he reads, stop him gently and remind him to use them. It can also be fun to assign a character to your child—ask her to read the heroine's lines as they come up.

Be sure to read along silently as your child reads aloud. You may need to help your child if he struggles with a word or phrase. You might even find it necessary to say the words aloud along with your child, using a low tone beneath his. This can help some children feel more confident and keep a flow to the text when they run up against troublesome or unfamiliar words. It enables comprehension and understanding of the story, while supporting and encouraging your child's own efforts.

A key factor in reading with your child is your own attitude:

Although it is not always easy, try to be as positive as possible. As your child struggles along, allow her to take her time. For example, don't become impatient with her if she appears to be stumbling over a word you just went over, or make her feel nervous by forcing her to guess how to sound it out. She should feel comfortable saying "I don't know what this is," and feel secure enough to take the risk of trying to sound out the word or use context clues to figure out what it means. It is crucial, therefore, to schedule reading sessions at a time when both you and your child are relaxed, comfortable, and happy. If evenings are rushed and frazzled at your house, don't wait until the end of the day. Sunrise reading time can be perfect for a family of "morning people," for example. Be creative in choosing the right time for you; if you have to borrow or buy two copies of every book and read "together" by phone during your afternoon coffee break, so be it.

CHOOSING THE RIGHT BOOKS FOR YOUR CHILD'S READING LEVEL

Whenever possible, let your child choose his own reading materials at the library or bookstore (with your supervision, of course). If he is drawn to a book, so much the better! Allow plenty of time for browsing, and encourage your child to look at several pages of the book, rather than choosing one based on a title or cover image. Look for these three elements inside the book:

➤ Pictures. In general, the higher the reading level, the fewer the pictures. For example, a second-grade-level book might have one picture for every four pages, while a beginning-reader book might have one on every page. But use your discretion: some picture books are created with an older audience in mind and may contain concepts beyond a young child's interest or understanding.

➤ Chapters. Chapter books are usually introduced to children gradually, starting sometime in the first grade, with books that are essentially short-story collections. In *Little Bear* by Else Homeland Minaret, for example, each chapter is a self-contained story and can be read without regard to the rest of the book. This is a hallmark of any chapter book aimed at early readers. A short novel—that is, a book-length story told over the course of several chapters—is usually thought to be at a second-grade level. So the more chapters in a book, the higher the level; if chapters are interlinked to form a single story, the book may be at a higher level still.

➤ Words per page. Beginning readers can find it hard to follow long paragraphs. They lose their place easily if called to read more than four or five lines on a single page. A book with an average of more than fifty words per page is probably at a second-grade level or higher.

Take *all* these factors into account as you evaluate a particular book.

Most children won't voluntarily pick a book that is far beyond their level of comprehension—few of us seek out failure or frustration—unless the subject is one of passionate interest to them. In these cases, be willing to go along for the read. It's worth it.

Hiding in Plain Sight

There are many ways to gauge a book's reading level. You could count the number of words on the average page; evaluate the difficulty of the vocabulary by tallying the number of multi-syllabic words, or tote up chapters and illustrations. You might steer you child toward book series that are strictly categorized as "Easy-to-Read," "Ready-to-Read," "I Can Read," and so on. Or you could just look for the codes on the back cover.

It's a little-known fact (among many parents, at any rate) that most of the companies that publish books for young people include a coded reading level or age level, and sometimes both, on their books. HarperTrophy, Dell Yearling, Avon Camelot, Scholastic, and Puffin are just a few of the prominent publishers that quantify their books' reading level, but don't make it obvious to consumers. (Applause goes to William Morrow's Beech Tree and Simon & Schuster's Aladdin imprints, which unashamedly highlight most of their books' suggested age ranges.)

If you're having a hard time figuring out whether a book will be too easy or too hard for your child to enjoy, the publisher's code might come in handy. Here's how to find it.

1. Get a paperback edition of the book. (Hardcover books and mass-market paperbacks don't usually carry the code.)

2. Turn it over. Toward the bottom of the back cover you'll see a bar code.

3. To one side of the bar code is the name of the publishing imprint and sometimes the symbol (or colophon) of the publisher.

4. Beneath the imprint name there may be several lines of codes and cover credits.

5. Look here for an RL (Reading Level) code, such as "RL 1.8". That's the reading level that the publisher has given the book. RL 1.8 means "the eighth month of the first-grade year": a reader of average skill will be able to read and comprehend this book in May of the first grade. RL 2.4 places the book at the reading level of an average second grader in January, and so on.

6. Above, beneath, or alongside the RL code—or all by itself—may be an unexplained series of four or six numerals. This is a suggested age range for the book. It may appear as "0508" or "005–008" (both mean "ages 5 to 8"). You'll occasionally see a number-word combination code, such as "10up." Very occasionally the word "Ages" will appear with this code as well, but not so prominantly that the average reader would notice.

Of course, age ranges and reading levels are subjective things—a book at almost any reading level may engage a child, depending on the subject, the story, and the author's skill. Still, it's something of a mystery why so many publishers rate their books this way . . . and then hide the information.

Libraries

Enlist the help of the children's librarians at your local public library. These well-trained professionals have literally made it their life's work to help kids find books. They will have plenty of ideas for reading materials that will appeal to your child on his own level—books, story collections, magazines, on-line resources, and more. In conversation, children's librarians are often skilled at drawing out children's interests and reading tastes. If your child is a reluctant reader, try to coax him into asking a librarian for help.

Other Resources

And while libraries are wonderful resources, there's something uniquely comfortable about reading a book of your very own. Your child deserves to have a personal book collection to savor, re-read, and enjoy. Get in the habit of giving books as gifts for birthdays and holidays. Bookstore personnel can make great book recommendations. Search out the independent children's book-stores in your area, as well as the children's sections in large general-interest stores (but be aware that bookstores devoted to children's literature are likely to have employees with more specialized knowledge of the genre). Don't overlook used-book outlets, especially if you're on a budget. Book catalogs, such as Chinaberry, newspapers such as the Sunday edition of the *New York Times*, children's magazines such as *Cricket* and *Lady Bug*, as well as trade publications such as *Publisher's Weekly*, *Booklist*, and *Kirkus Reviews* often contain extensive reviews that can give you an excellent feel for a title. Online resources, such as amazon.com, post lists of favorite books by age group, as well as helpful and informative book reviews. You can also find a list of children's bestsellers, which are a great way to find books that are likely to appeal to your child. If you are still uncertain about a title, read a customer review from those who have already read the book.

Kids who are struggling with reading may choose books that seem far below their level of ability. If your child zips through a book without stopping to sound out or reconsider any words at all, it's probably too easy for her. You can try to steer her gently toward more challenging material. ("Maybe we can borrow that book so you can read it to your baby sister. How about this one for you?") But don't force the issue: an "easy" book that she can read on her own may be just what your child needs to boost her self-confidence at this point. When fear of failure is an issue, "too easy" is certainly better than nothing at all.

Some of our favorite easy reader titles include:

- *Where the Wild Things Are* by Maurice Sendak (for emerging readers)
- *If You Give a Pig a Pancake* by Laura J. Numeroff (for first graders)
- *Junie B. Jones and Some Sneaky Peeky Spying* by Barbara Park (for second graders)

EVALUATING YOUR CHILD'S READING PROGRESS

Effective evaluation is as individual as your child. Be sure to ask your child's teacher for particular milestones to watch out for. Some of these may include:

- ➤ Can decode a new word on sight
- ➤ Can tell the setting, simple plot, and characters of a story
- ➤ Can read a never before seen appropriate-level book

For general motivation and encouragement (your child's and your own), maintain some kind of regular record of your child's reading work. You can use a small notebook to keep a simple "reading journal" together.

November 17

Brianna read *Green Eggs and Ham* by herself.

November 18

We looked at *Nickelodeon Magazine* together, and Brianna pointed to all the words she could recognize.

November 20

At the supermarket, Brianna helped by reading items from the list for Mommy. She read *Brown Bear, Brown Bear* to her brother as a bedtime story.

Books We Read in November

Corduroy
  by Don Freeman

In the Small, Small Pond
  by Denise Fleming

Green Eggs and Ham
  by Dr. Seuss

Brown Bear, Brown Bear, What Do You See?
  by Bill Martin and Eric Carle

Miss Spider's Tea Party
  by David Kirk

Jessica
  by Kevin Henkes

You can also use your reading journal as a place for both you and your child to record your reactions to the books you read together. Write down how the book or chapter you shared made you feel, what you thought of the characters, whether it reminded you of another story, or that you didn't like the ending—whatever your response may have been. Reading journals encourage kids to become critical readers and gently push them toward improvements in comprehension. Over time, the journal entries will give you a clear picture of your child's expanding skills.

If your child enjoys being the center of attention, try videotaping or audiotaping your child reading a few pages aloud. Do this regularly—every two weeks or so—and you'll both be able to see and hear exactly how well your child is doing.

COMMON READING PROBLEMS

It's important to know a bit about the kinds of problems your child may be experiencing now—as well as the elements of reading that are *not* causing her trouble.

First of all, rest assured that your child is not alone. While percentages vary from district to district and from school to school, it's not unusual for 15 to 50 percent of children in the first and second grades to have some kind of delay in their reading progress.

Comprehension Problems

Probably the most common reading problem among first- and second-graders involves comprehension—understanding the text on various levels. Frequently, children read words individually, and find it hard to put them all together in a way that gives any meaning to what they have just read.

Decoding Problems

If your child has trouble decoding—sounding out—unfamiliar words, does not associate letters with the sounds they make, or has trouble blending letter sounds together, she's experiencing a phonetic delay. A simple flash card quiz (see Chapter 4), conducted at home in a low-key atmosphere, can give you some idea of the dimension of your child's phonics skills: if she is not associating letters with the sounds they make, some remedial, foundational phonics learning is in order.

If your child understands how letters and letter sounds relate but is having trouble linking sounds together to form whole words, give her an unfamiliar book and ask her to read it to you. Again, try to avoid any feeling of urgency or pressure. If she is reluctant to sound out unknown words or makes wild guesses instead of reading them, she may need to work on blends and general decoding skills.

Working on phonics is as essential to reading as rules are to any game. You wouldn't send your child out to play soccer without telling her that the idea is to get the ball in the other team's goal and that she has to use her feet to get it there. In the same way, phonetic rules are the framework of reading, and your child can't "play the game" without them.

Physical Problems

One of the first things you should do when you discover that your child is having trouble in school is to take him to the pediatrician for a complete physical exam. Hearing, speech, and vision problems should be investigated when a child isn't reading on level. Your child may need more sleep, or a change in diet. The learning delay may even be a symptom of an otherwise silent illness, such as a blood disorder, or a newly developed allergy. The effects of past health problems, such as frequent ear infections in your child's earlier years, may only be showing up now. Be sure to rule out all possible physical causes of the problem. Follow up with hearing, vision, or other specialists as needed.

Children can be extraordinarily skilled at compensating for physical problems, to the point where even those closest to them never suspect that anything is wrong. A child with hearing loss, for example, can learn to read lips, or if he has double vision may use only one eye at a time. These coping strategies are frequently subconscious. The child may be so used to dealing with his problem that he simply doesn't recognize it as a problem. However, it might be at the root of his academic difficulty.

Diet Matters:

What—and *when*—your child eats during the day can also have a noticeable effect on his attention span and capacity to learn. Food and mood are more closely linked in some children than others. Ask the classroom teacher whether your child is eating a snack in the morning. If so, when? If snack time is scheduled an hour after your child has finished breakfast, his dramatic change in blood sugar levels might be causing problems for him. A simple switch to low-sugar snack foods or a change in eating time might make a difference. Check with your child's pediatrician or a nutritionist.

Allergies can also have subtle effects on a child's ability to concentrate and learn. Seasonal allergies, that peak at crucial points in the school year, can be particularly troublesome. Again, this is something your pediatrician or an allergist may need to look into.

WHAT YOU CAN DO TO HELP

As a parent, there's a lot you can do to help your child deal with reading difficulties. First of all, meet the problem head-on; calmly but with as much confidence as you can muster. It may be that your child has a need for specialized instruction, or her difficulties may be addressed by adjusting her diet or the time she goes to bed. Regardless, your child *will* improve with a little effort on everyone's part.

➤ *Phonics work* is typically the first course of attack when a reading problem emerges. Frequently, the classroom teacher will take the initiative and give special assignments to help a struggling child catch up to her peers. The teacher might also provide her with supplemental phonics work sheets, phonics games, and flash cards. If you can pin your child's problem down as phonics-related, an investment in a home phonics program may be part of the solution. Programs like *Hooked On Phonics* and *The Phonics Game* can be effective for a child needing work in this area. If you own a home PC and your child enjoys computer games, you may be able to get her to "learn through play" with arcade-like educational software like *Reader Rabbit* or *Reading Blaster*. (See Chapter 9 for more on these programs.)

➤ *Reading support* is the route to take if comprehension is your child's trouble spot. Some children need motivation and encouragement to get into the habit of reading, as well as practice in such reading-related skills as sequencing, prediction, and inference. (See Chapter 6 for more information.) Reading support is something that most parents can undertake at home. Start by modeling good reading habits: pick up a new book yourself, or read the daily newspaper.

➤ Some families have adopted the Drop Everything And Read (DEAR) method, in which a half-hour of each day is set aside for everyone in the house to stop what they are doing and pick up a book to do just that.

➤ Game playing can also work wonders. Many of the activities described in Chapter 6 are, in effect, reading support exercises. By playing a game of Junior Scrabble your child will learn to spell and read words on her own.

➤ *Tutoring* is a good solution in many cases. Some children need one-on-one instruction and feedback to make reading progress, which can be difficult to get in schools that are understaffed or have large class sizes. A child who is prone to distraction or daydreams in a group setting will benefit greatly from tutoring sessions. So will a child who lacks confidence or fears failure. A tutor can offer discipline, encouragement, support, structure, instant responses, and tailored programming as the individual student needs it. For a young reader, that can make all the difference. (See Chapter 8 for more on the tutoring relationship and how to make it work.)

➤ *Special programs* are offered in many schools for students who are struggling with reading. Remedial reading teachers may work on phonics or comprehension with a few children at a time in a small group setting. Or an international program like Reading Recovery may be available. Reading Recovery is an intervention system used with first-graders who are running into reading roadblocks. Because it calls for specially trained teachers to work one-on-one with students, its adoption calls for considerable investment on the part of the school or district. But for thousands of children worldwide who have blossomed into skilled readers with the help of the program, it's a worthwhile investment. (See Chapter 9 for more on the program.)

ONE STEP BACK—ONE GIANT LEAP AHEAD

Although you may be reluctant to consider it an alternative, the best thing for your child may be to repeat the school year. Some children are just not ready to be promoted, even if they are being tutored and receive lots of extra support at home. Sometimes they need another year to grow, expand, and gain more life experience. It's a difficult message to convey to parents whose child is struggling, but a set back is often the most important ingredient in encouraging a student to go on to future success. Holding back can help, because in the repeat year the child starts to see grades he can be proud of and say "I did it on my own." Whatever came before no longer matters, now he has succeeded. This, in turn, will fuel his enthusiasm and drive him forward.

TAKING THE FIRST STEPS

If you've heard, through a mid-term note or during a regular parent-teacher conference, that your child is falling behind her class in reading skills, now is the time to take action. Here are ten things you can do right away to start your child on a fresh academic path.

1. Schedule a conference with your child's teacher so you can talk in depth about your child's particular problem. (See Chapter 3 for more on how to make the most of parent/teacher meetings.)

2. Begin a regular at-home reading routine. Start today, with an old favorite, so your child can read along with you easily and comfortably. Remember, success in reading encourages further success. Give your child an immediate reward for sticking with his reading routine. Give him a fun sticker to put on a simple chart after each reading session is complete so he can have a visible reminder of his on-going progress.

3. Work a library visit into your weekly schedule. Set aside enough time to talk to the librarian for tips and recommendations. Browse through several books before choosing which ones to take home with you. Read a few pages with your child to make sure the level is right and the interest is there. Let your child get her own library card—a point of pride for many beginning readers. (And if you don't have a library card yourself, now's the time!)

4. Take your child to a park, your back yard, or an empty lot and observe together one living thing. Follow an ant; dig up a worm. Help your child write her observations down, or have her draw a detailed picture of what she saw.

5. Cook a simple dish (or batch of his favorite cookies) with your child's assistance. Have him read the recipe, measure the ingredients, or follow your directions. Experiential learning activities like these are great ways to sharpen your child's understanding of sequencing, cause and effect, inference, prediction, vocabulary, and more. (Additional activities in this vein are featured in Chapter 6.)

6. Set up a special "Homework Zone" with your child's help (see Chapter 4 for ideas).

7. Turn off the TV for a full hour. Then do it again tomorrow.

8. Prepare for your parent-teacher meeting by quietly observing your child's reading attempts for a few days beforehand. You may spot some useful clues this way. Is your child squinting at the page? Easily distracted? Rushing through material? Is the atmosphere quiet and peaceful? (See Chapter 3 for more tips and a worksheet you can use to focus your observations.)

9. Give some thought to your daily household schedule so that you'll come away from the meeting with a do-able action plan. Be realistic: if your work schedule only leaves you twenty minutes a night to read with your child, both you and the teacher will need to be aware of that. Remember that even small steps will help get your child moving in the right direction. Visit a teachers' store in your area, or check out some of the many Internet sites that offer teaching materials, to become familiar with the kinds of workbooks, card sets, and other aids that are available at your child's level. You may be surprised at the wide array of materials that are designed to support his at-home reading program. (Chapter 9 lists some of the leading national teacher's stores and web sites. Check your local telephone directory for outlets close to home.)

Educators agree that regular and active parental involvement is a key component to a child's success in grade school, and even beyond. Your participation in your child's education is never more critical than now, when she is learning to read. Indeed, the most important educational goal for your first- or second-grader is to become completely comfortable with words.

The process is complicated, but this chapter has shown what practical steps can be taken to help your child become a successful reader. It explores how children learn and encourages parents to form a partnership with their children's teachers. It offers important information about the methods used to teach reading, gives tips on how to choose the right books for your child's reading level, and shows how to evaluate your child's reading progress. Chapter 1 also covered the tremendously important subject of common reading problems and what you, as a parent, can do to help solve them.

Throughout these pages and in those that follow the emphasis is on making the process of learning to read exciting, joyful, and purposeful. Therefore, do not be discouraged if you discover that your child needs more help than you or her school can provide. Outside resources, such as tutors or learning programs may be exactly what she needs to become a satisfied and successful reader. Chapters 7 and 8 offer information and insights into understanding, evaluating, and choosing additional help. Chapter 2 takes parents into school and explains what the reading expectations are for first and second graders. Here you'll learn more about the most positive and constructive ways to support your budding reader and how to understand the role of standardized tests and the reasoning behind "teaching to the test."

Reading is a skill that is nothing short of miraculous: A passport to knowledge, imagination, opportunity, art, and the wider world, it opens the door to a lifetime of learning. For almost everyone, reading is a prime factor in leading a successful life. And in the more circumscribed world of school—your child's world right now—reading success *is* success, to a very large degree. Without knowing how to read most of us simply would not be able to function. Can you imagine living in our world without being able to read directions, fill out a job application or follow instructions on a bottle of medicine? Reading is ingrained in our lives. It is as palpable as weather or the streets we walk on—even the online world is basically a text environment.

2

A School's-Eye View

▼

You can count on the fact that your child's teacher wants your child to succeed just as much as you do. It's a matter of professional pride. It's also a practical imperative: many teachers—and schools—are evaluated and rewarded on the basis of their students' scores on particular statewide or local assessment tests. To that end elementary schools across the country are "teaching to the test" as early as kindergarten.

But before you begin to worry about the impact of a state or locally mandated agenda on your child's educational future, read on. You may be surprised to learn that necessity is, indeed, the mother of invention, even—and perhaps especially—when it comes to primary education.

This chapter fills you in on the basic skills your first or second grader is expected to acquire as a beginning reader. Then it discusses the terms and philosophies of reading that are currently in use—phonics and whole language—and explains the balance that most reading teachers have come to adopt in their classrooms.

Finally, you may discover that although educational debates come and go the latest imperative to "teach to the test" has given rise to a raft of successful methods of teaching children to read. "Graphic organizers," such as Venn diagrams, story and sequence maps, and word webs are a few of the analytical tools that are giving children the skills to read with greater comprehension and enjoyment. Scores, it turns out, are only part of a much bigger and more inventive picture.

Reading Terms

Every profession has its own jargon, and teaching is no exception. To work with your child's teacher comfortably, you need a working knowledge of the reading-related terms you're likely to hear her use. Here are some of the most important ones:

Basal reader: A term used by teachers that refers to a book used as a reading textbook.

Blend: A consonant pair that makes a sound in which both letters can be heard: "bl," "br," "st," "sk."

Cause and effect: A story or sentence that demonstrates how the events of a story relate to each other, e.g. the parade was cancelled because it was raining.

Context clues: Understanding the meaning of a word based on the information around it.

Decoding: The process of using phonemes to read or pronounce new words.

Digraph: A consonant pair that combines to make a single sound in which neither source letter can be distinguished: "th," "sh," "ch."

Diphthong: (same definition as digraph)

Guided questions: Questions that are intended to guide a student's thought process.

Inference: Occurs when a reader makes an assumption based on information other than an explicit statement, such as "Annie was laughing." A student can infer that Annie is happy; even though she has not been told "Annie is happy."

Modeling: Teaching a concept by putting it into action. For example, parents who read books at home are modeling good reading habits for their children.

Phonics: A method of teaching beginners to read and pronounce words by learning the phonetics of letters, letter groups, and syllables.

Phoneme: The smallest unit of sound. For example, the word CAT has three phonemes: kuh-ah-tuh.

Prediction: A thought process used by readers to guess what is likely to happen next in a story.

Reversals: Occur when beginning readers (and writers) reverse letters, such as "b" and "d."

Sequencing: The reading comprehension skill that allows readers to understnad logical progression and order within a story or text.

Sight vocabulary: The totality of words one can read at a single glance, without the use of any decoding skills or context clues.

Strategic reading: All the skills one brings to bear when using a text to answer a specific question.

Venn diagram: A diagram that employs circles to represent a relationship between two or more items by inclusion, exclusion, and intersection.

Whole language: A method of teaching children to read through the recognition of whole words, not letters and syllables.

Word webbing: A graphic organization method that links a main idea and its supporting details into an interconnected spiderweb pattern.

FIRST-GRADE EXPECTATIONS

In the primary grades, reading and writing can easily take up half of every school day. So, even though your child will be learning math, science, and social studies this year, and will likely take in a smattering of art, music, computers, and health, her main preoccupation will be learning the foundational skills relating to language.

At some point during her year in first grade, your child will be expected to:

➤ Understand that words carry meaning
➤ Comprehend cues such as punctuation marks, capitalization, and titles
➤ Show a literal understanding of a story by answering factual questions about plot and character
➤ Use a "sight vocabulary" of at least 300 words
➤ Recognize rhyming words and word families
➤ Begin to use expression when reading aloud
➤ Read and follow simple written instructions
➤ Plan a writing project, with adult help as needed

➤ Draft sentences using "creative" or "temporary" spelling
➤ Revise and correct written work
➤ Present written work to others

The early months of first grade are given over to reviews of the alphabet, the difference between vowels and consonants, and simple words. Although the focus is on decoding skills at the beginning of the year, comprehension gradually comes into play over the ensuing months. By November, children are using simple sequencing, identifying the main idea of a sentence, and determining cause and effect. At the same time, their decoding skills become progressively more sophisticated. Many teachers use the concept of "word families" to demonstrate how vowels and consonants can be combined into patterns to make new words. As students learn to match short vowels and then long vowels with beginning and ending consonant sounds, they master more and more words that they can read on their own.

Students' writing abilities should be honed and practiced throughout the year. By the end of first grade your child should be able to write a paragraph-long story (about four to five sentences long).

By June first graders are expected to speak and be understood through clear and concise language. They should be able to express complete thoughts and report on a topic. By the end of the year they are also expected to pick out library books that are suitable for their reading level and write two or three sentences on a given topic. Punctuation and spelling should be correct. However, if a child cannot spell every word correctly, he should know how to use a dictionary or refer to other sources that might give him the information he needs. Other year-end expectations include:

➤ Knowing the difference between short and long vowels, and the difference between consonants and vowels
➤ Differentiating a noun from a verb
➤ Constructing a sentence with a "naming part" (or subject) and an "action part" (or predicate)
➤ Reading a book of a certain length—depending on the child's reading level—from beginning to end, and reporting on it

SECOND-GRADE EXPECTATIONS

The continued development of language skills is also a huge part of the second-grade curriculum, although there's a stronger emphasis on advanced comprehension skills. Your child will be expected to use strategies such as prediction, inference, cause-and-effect, and critical thinking to understand reading material more deeply than before. He will also be asked to produce longer pieces of writing, such as book reports and stories.

During his year as a second grader, your child should be able to:

➤ Use comprehension skills before, during, and after reading
➤ Recall the sequence of events in a story
➤ Draw simple, logical conclusions from reading material
➤ Identify cause and effect relationships
➤ Rely on print more than illustrations for meaning
➤ Connect details and events in a story to his own experiences
➤ Use phonics to understand new words
➤ Independently use graphic organizers to plan a writing project
➤ Use graphic organizers to draft sentences
➤ Use classroom reference materials to make corrections
➤ Produce a variety of reports, stories, and summaries
➤ Identify and choose resource materials to research a topic

By the end of second grade, students should have a thorough comprehension of what they read, as well as the ability to read independently. Even if a second grader comes across a word she has never seen before, she should be able to decode it, using phonics skills mastered over the course of the year. These skills, combined with context clues should facilitate independent reading. While first-grade-level stories are meant to be read and understood in a literal sense, second graders are expected to become sensitized to the nuances and meaning of a story. Digging a little deeper for details and getting a more thorough understanding of what they're reading shouldn't be too much of a struggle for most second graders, especially if they've already mastered the fundamentals of phonics. Where your six year old might have answered a question with a single word, your second grader now eagerly answers questions in complete sentences. Or at least he does sometimes!

PHILOSOPHIES OF READING

So much discussion of what is expected of first and second graders leads up to one question: how *do* you teach reading to a child, anyway? It's a simple query, but there isn't a simple answer.

Phonics

The term "phonics" refers to individual letter sounds—phonemes—that readers use to understand complete words. Most of us would describe phonics as a process of "sounding out a word," although an educator might refer to it as "decoding."

Phonics requires a thorough understanding of each letter of the alphabet, the sounds that they make, and the combinations of sounds they can form. Once students know the sounds that letters make, they can put those sounds together to understand words.

DOG

duh + au + guh

dog

All of this sounds simple enough, but there's a catch: the English language is inconsistent at best in matters of spelling, and the letters of our alphabet don't always behave predictably. Vowels can be pronounced with both long and short sounds, and even some consonants have different sounds in different words.

C A T

kuh (but not suh) + ah (but not ay) + tuh

cat

Then there are sounds made by letters in combination, which have a whole set of their own rules that readers must learn. The fact that s + h = "sh" or n + g = "ing" is not intuitively grasped. It has to be taught—over and over again—throughout the early years of one's reading life. Learning phonics doesn't stop in the first or second grade; it can take years of constant review and use before some concepts are fully absorbed and internalized. Some students may not really understand the long vowel, for example, until the third grade. They may have heard about it for two years, but they haven't really 'learned' it until they can recognize—and use—it on their own. Proponents of phonics argue that their teaching methods give children the tools to understand any word in the English language and provide a framework on which an extensive vocabulary can be built.

But critics point to the difficulty of engaging some students with phonics. Learning letter sounds is unexciting at best, and forcing rote memorization on children so early in their school careers could turn some of them off to education altogether. Hook kids on *reading*, they say, not on the nuts and bolts of the process. To do that, surround them with exciting words: literature.

Whole Language

The whole language method grew out of the very accurate observation that good readers recognize complete words, not the individual letters within them. As you read this sentence, you're probably not stopping to sound out every word as you go. You see "word" and understand the idea, rather than thinking "wuh + uh + ruh + duh = word."

From the concept "good readers read words, not letters" grew the notion that surrounding children with words would naturally speed them towards becoming good readers themselves, with a minimum of fuss and no drilling at all.

Thus a "whole language classroom" is awash in words. Objects are labeled, books are everywhere, and the written word is used extensively to teach every subject, including math, music, and art. Even the youngest students are encouraged to write and use "creative spelling" to express their ideas freely. At the same time, their reading materials are filled with pictures that help them understand stories and pick up more and more words as they go.

The whole language method gives children early training and practice in comprehension techniques through a heavy emphasis on reading experiences that use context to derive meaning. Since most students' reading problems are rooted in comprehension difficulties rather than phonetic delays, whole reading methods undoubtedly have an advantage.

Indeed, whole-language proponents argue that the overall quirkiness of the English language makes a devotion to phonics rather pointless. With so many hundreds of exceptions to the rules of English-language phonics, why teach the rules at all? Wouldn't it be better to expose students to as many words as possible throughout the day, give them books loaded with pictures as context clues, ask them to follow the words as they are being read to, and help them recognize complete words for what they are? As her "sight vocabulary"—the list of words she can recognize instantly—expands, the student will be able to read more and more independently, and will be encouraged to read because of her long immersion in the world of words.

But critics compare the whole language approach to a meal that begins with dessert—an exciting reversal that might stimulate children's palates, but ultimately gives them less than a balanced diet. Whole language may help children enjoy school, the critics maintain, but it simply does not teach them how to actually read. In fact, some children come home and tell their parents that they don't know how. Then, when mom or dad suggests "sounding out" words in order to read them (after all that was how *they* were taught), the unarticulated answer frequently is "What do you mean sound it out? I just look at the word and expose myself to the surrounding vocabulary and that's how I learn what the word is." Unfortunately, for most students this system doesn't work.

THE SOLUTION

Thankfully, the "reading wars" seem to be abating in most parts of the country, as teachers on the front lines make the sensible choice to embrace elements of both approaches in their classrooms. Most level-headed teachers don't jump on any bandwagon; they take the best of both approaches and incorporate phonics and whole language into their classrooms. In the end, it is the most inclusive approach, because if you don't teach phonics, children who aren't receptive to a whole-language style of teaching are not going to learn how to read. And if you just teach phonics and don't bring in other literature to your methods, children will not be exposed to different writing styles or a larger vocabulary. So both are needed in order to have a complete program.

To that end, many primary-grade teachers strive to make their classrooms feel "reading-friendly" with classroom libraries, numerous labels, writing centers, and other features. They allow for independent reading time during the school day and encourage the class to read materials other than the textbook by assigning book reports of various kinds—oral, written, acted, or drawn. They also incorporate writing and reading into every aspect of the curriculum: for example, students may be asked to write an essay as part of a science lesson, devise a word problem for math, or create a museum label for the painting they made in art class. But all of this occurs while a broad range of decoding skills is being introduced and reinforced.

HOW TEACHERS TEACH READING

Decoding skills are the framework of reading, an essential structural element. But a house is not a house when only the wooden frame has been raised. Think of comprehension skills as the walls, roof, appliances, and furniture of the house. You can't move in until all these things are in place, too.

Decoding Skills

The twenty-six letters of the alphabet are divided into vowels and consonants. The vowels are A, E, I, O, U. The consonants are the remaining twenty-one letters. Together consonants and vowels are the source of the forty-four sounds created by the English alphabet. Vowels may have a long sound such as the E in "tree" or a short sound such as the letter I in "kick." Children are taught the long and short sounds of each vowel:

A—long "ay" or short "ah," as in gate vs. bat
E—long "ee" or short "eh," as in tree vs. pet
I—long "ai" or short "ih," as in pipe vs. kick
O—long "oh" or short "aw," as in boat vs. pot
U—long "ooh" or short "uh," as in cute vs. but

Some consonants also have different sounds. They can be hard or soft. Take the letter G for example: it can be hard if it is followed by a, i, o, or u, as in gate, gift, got, or gut, while it can be soft if it is followed by e or y, as in gel, or gym.

The names and sounds of the letters of the alphabet are introduced to most children in kindergarten, if not before. By first grade, teachers expect students to be intimately familiar with all twenty-six letters. Your child should now be able to name at least two or three words that begin with each letter, and should be able to tell you the primary sound that each letter makes, without any hesitation.

In the early part of the year, first-grade teachers spend a lot of classroom time reviewing the letters and their sounds, often in a sing-song alphabet drill: "A, ah; B, buh; C, cuh; D, duh . . ." As the review continues, the teacher shows the class how some of those sounds can be combined to create a simple three-letter word. She will typically demonstrate with an initial consonant sound, like "buh," before a short vowel sound, such as "ah," followed by an ending consonant sound, like "tuh." The students can then learn to blend the sounds together to form a word—"buh-ah-tuh, bat." The whole process is repeated for each of the short-vowel sounds and then for all the long-vowel sounds.

Decoding gets considerably trickier as students move on to more complex words. The English language is notoriously difficult to spell, because our words have been adapted from so many different source languages and follow so many obscure rules. (Compare the words "weigh" and "laugh," for instance, and imagine how bizarre they must look to a young reader.) Teachers try to give their students some help along the way with short-vowel, long-vowel, and consonant rules that they can generally rely on for decoding purposes. For example:

➤ When one vowel appears between two consonants, the vowel usually says its short sound.
➤ If there is an e at the end of a word, the vowel sound is long and the e is not pronounced—it's silent.
➤ A vowel before a doubled consonant says its short sound.
➤ When two vowels appear together, we usually hear only the first vowel, and it says its long sound (or, "When two vowels go walking, the first does the talking").
➤ When a word has only one vowel and it appears at the end of the word, it usually says its long sound.
➤ When c or g comes immediately before a, o, or u, we say its hard sound.
➤ When c or g comes immediately before e, i, or y, we say its soft sound.

But of course, there are many exceptions to every one of the rules—so many that you can probably come up with an exception to every rule in the list, right off the top of your head. Learning the exceptions will only come with time and reading experience. No wonder so many young readers struggle!

Working with word "families" is an effective element in any system of teaching decoding skills, as well as a common technique in teaching spelling. Word families are groups of rhyming words that are spelled similarly. A word family offers a pattern, such as the "-at" sound. The student can then build on the pattern with various initial letters or sounds to name any number of words in the "-at family": bat, cat, sat, hat, mat, pat, that, chat, splat, and so on.

Once a child understands how the family pattern works, he'll find it easy to recognize and read all the related words. It's a tremendous confidence-booster for a new reader to be able to look at a list of unfamiliar but related words and read them all. It's one reason why rhyme is such an important element in so many children's books. In the same way, it's a thrill for young writers to be able to correctly spell lists of words in a family.

But again, even rhyming words can play tricks. The words "wait" and "bait" are in the "ait" family, but the sound-alike "mate" and "hate" are in the "ate" family. Again, only reading experience, extensive exposure to these and many other words, will get a reader past these stumbling blocks.

Many teachers have developed their own methods of introducing and reinforcing the rules and exceptions of phonics, from flash card drills to in-class phonics contests. See Chapter 5 for a unique phonetic spelling technique that you can easily practice at home.

Comprehension Skills

For all its importance, phonics is useless without understanding. And so decoding and comprehension skills must go hand in hand. Without using both a child isn't really reading.

Simply put, reading comprehension is the ability to link words together into sentences and to understand the idea that the author is trying to convey in those sentences. It's a complex skill that involves a number of discrete tasks, including inference, the ability to make logical leaps between the reading material and other facts known to the reader; sequencing, the recognition of order and process within the work being read; prediction, the ability to anticipate what will happen next in a story; and more.

Part of a child's ability to comprehend reading material is a simple matter of life experience. It's difficult to understand any concept if you've had no direct experience of it, or if you've never even heard of it before. Adults have the benefit of years of personal and second-hand knowledge to draw on whenever they read a story or article. On some level, we are constantly comparing what we read and hear against our storehouse of memory to understand, evaluate, and place things in context. A young reader has a much more limited memory bank, and so comprehension is much harder work for her. That's why it's so important for parents to expose their children to as much life experience as they can—by going places and seeing things together, working around the house together, observing the natural world together, and reading together, too.

> 66 Many parents are overly focused on the *words*. Some come into the classroom saying "My child can read." And they're right: their children can read certain words. But when you ask them what they mean, the children don't know. That's not reading. That's saying words. 99
>
> —A FIRST-GRADE TEACHER FROM NEW JERSEY

It's also why teachers work so hard with children to help them analyze, organize, and understand everything they read in school. Graphic organizers are popular comprehension aids that many teachers are using in their classrooms. The QAR strategy is another. QAR—"Question and Answer Reading"—asks students to answer four types of questions as they read a story. The questions, known as "right there," "think and search," "on my own," and "author and you," steer young readers toward finding answers within the reading material and from their own reactions to what they've read.

> ➤ A "right there" question is on the literal level and asks the reader to uncover a simple fact from the text. "Where was Little Red Riding Hood going?" is a "right there" question.
> ➤ A "think and search" question also operates on a literal level, but it requires the reader to look in more than one place in the text to find the answer. "Why was Little Red Riding Hood going to visit her grandmother?" is an example.
> ➤ An "on my own" question asks readers to make inferences between the story and their own ideas or experiences, such as "Have you ever gone to visit your grandmother or grandfather?"
> ➤ "Author and you" questions get readers to see the story from a critical perspective. For example, "What did the author want us to understand about being careful?"

QAR techniques, organizing methods, and long-term assignments like book reports and presentations all reinforce comprehension skills in the classroom. At home, children can work on comprehension very naturally through conversation about books, experiences of the world around them, and imaginative games of many kinds. See Chapter 6 for ideas.

The Classroom Environment

Depending on the teacher's style and perhaps school rules, classroom accoutrements can clue you in to the kind of learning that's being encouraged there. A "reading-friendly" classroom helps makes children comfortable with the world of books. Is your child's classroom one of them? Look for:

> 66Comprehension skills depend to some extent on students' backgrounds, what experiences they've had, how much they can bring to the story. Say you read a story about a soccer game. Someone who's played soccer will have a better understanding of the story than someone who's never even seen a soccer ball. And that's why doing things with children at an early age is so important. Taking walks in the woods and going to the zoo and museums and baking together—all those things bring more experience to their lives, which they can then incorporate into their reading.99
>
> —A FIRST-GRADE TEACHER FROM NEW JERSEY

- ➤ A classroom library
- ➤ A read-aloud corner or rug
- ➤ A display of book reports and other reading-related responses
- ➤ Prompts such as long-vowel charts and vocabulary lists
- ➤ A "Featured Author" display with information on a favorite author or illustrator and a collection of that person's books
- ➤ An author's chair for students to use while reading their own work to the class
- ➤ Students actually engaged in reading
- ➤ A listening center with books on audiotape, tape players, and headphones
- ➤ A writing center with reference books and creative materials
- ➤ Labels on objects around the classroom
- ➤ Children's first and last names on tables, chairs, and cubbies
- ➤ A comfortable space for independent between-lesson reading

General classroom organization can vary widely in the first and second grades, from the classic single-desks-in-rows model to modular groupings of four or six desks. Another variation includes multi-level classrooms that combine children at two or more grade levels into a single class, and rely on learning stations and task-specific areas to keep several lessons going at once. But remember that a cutting-edge classroom is no guarantee of an effective education. Strong, creative teaching goes on in all kinds of environments. What should matter most to you is whether the surroundings will stimulate your child's learning process or hamper it. A child who is easily bored may thrive in a multi-level classroom, while a child who is easily distracted may find it impossible to learn in the same environment. Talk to your child, as well as her teacher, and visit the school during class time to get an idea of how the classroom functions. If you feel that a different learning atmosphere might help solve your child's problem, don't be shy about discussing it with the teacher or administration.

The division of classes by skills is called "tracking," and it's not an uncommon practice. In addition, there are schools that pull children out for certain subjects or simply group them for specific subjects by ability. There are educators who believe in tracking, and there are others who don't. The pros of tracking are that children may learn best when they are with other children with similar abilities, and teachers are better able to meet the needs of all the children in the class when skills aren't widely divergent. The cons of tracking are that a child's ranking may be based on only certain skills, while in actuality; the child has other skills in which he excels. Moreover, children's abilities can change over the course of the school year.

TEACHING FOR "THE TEST"

The 1990s saw a pronounced rise in the public's call for accountability in the education system. No longer content with passing grades and promoting students for social reasons, politicians and taxpayers began to demand proof of performance. The standardized test was back in vogue.

Standardized testing has been a familiar part of students' school careers for decades, thanks in large part to the Scholastic Aptitude Test and its role in college admissions. At the elementary school level, however, standardized tests have been used traditionally as evaluative tools to help teachers understand the strengths and weaknesses of individual students.

No more. Today, the results of grade-school standardized tests are made painfully public. For students, poor performance can mean summer school or a repeated grade; for teachers, it can mean the loss of professional pride or even advancement; for schools, it can mean the loss of accreditation, administrators' jobs, school board control, and community confidence.

And all this responsibility is carried on the small shoulders of third, fourth, or fifth graders over the course of two or three days of testing. Is it any wonder that schools nationwide are drilling children as early as kindergarten in the skills they need to do well on these tests?

Early Standardized Tests State by State

While not every state in the union test students in the first and second grade, here are some that do:

CALIFORNIA: The Stanford Achievement Test (SAT—not to be confused with the Scholastic Aptitude Test—tests second graders in Reading/Language Arts skills.

DISTRICT OF COLUMBIA: The nation's capital also uses the Stanford Achievement Test. Standardized reading tests are administered to both first and second graders.

SOUTH DAKOTA: This state uses a nationally standardized norm-referenced achievement and ability test. Second graders are tested in reading.

VERMONT: The Vermont Comprehensive Assessment System (VCAS) tests second graders in reading skills.

WEST VIRGINIA: The Statewide Assessment Program tests both first and second graders in Reading/Language Arts and listening skills.

Standardized tests become more common as your child reaches upper grades. Stay informed, ask your child's teacher when and if any additional standardized tests are given throughout the year. For complete information on standardized tests, see *A Parent's Guide to Standardized Tests in School*, by Peter W. Cookson, Ph. D.

But "teaching for the test" is an idea that carries deeply negative connotations for many educators and parents who worry that the emphasis on scores encourages a shallow focus on rote learning and test-taking skills, and sacrifices a deep understanding of concepts. Too much of an emphasis on "teaching for the test" leaves little room for "creative" teaching and learning, and puts limits on other facets of the curriculum. Consequently, very few teachers like to admit that they are actually "teaching for the test." For example, a teacher might say that he is "laying the groundwork for later success" (instead of "teaching with the test in mind") when he spends class time introducing children to Venn diagrams, reading-comprehension exercises, essay writing, or any other subject that is emphasized on state or local standardized tests. For a parent, this is a hair-splitting distinction. Either way, a future standardized test is affecting your child right now. You need to know how.

Graphic Organizers

Graphic organizing techniques are moving into all areas of the curriculum because of their increasing popularity as aids for children who are being prepared for the new essay-based standardized tests. In the "old days," you may have been taught the basic outline, a paragraph-by-paragraph plan for an essay or other written presentation. You may also remember the "Venn diagram" from your grammar-school math lessons: a pair of interlocking circles used to identify common elements within two separate sets.

In the past, though, Venn diagrams would only show up in math textbooks, usually as the hallmark of back-to-school lessons on set theory. Now it's a major teaching tool in reading and language arts lessons, not to mention social studies and science. Teachers use it to help students compare two characters in a story, analyze two versions of the same tale, evaluate two historical figures, or contrast the results of two experiments.

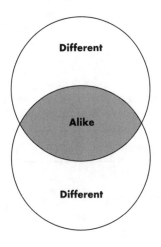

Today, with the new emphasis on reading comprehension and written communication in every subject area, graphic organizers have proliferated, almost becoming a study unto themselves. For example, there's the "story map," which helps students analyze the major elements—plot, character, and setting—of a work of fiction.

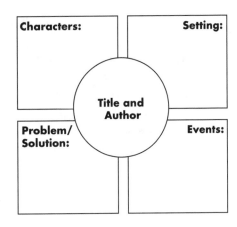

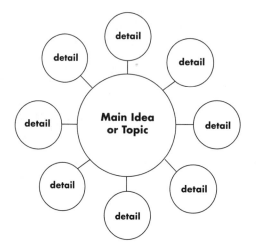

There's the "word web," a loose conceptual organizer that lends itself to brainstorming and other kinds of creative thinking. Here, a main idea or topic is written in the center of the web, and students are asked to free-associate about that topic to come up with other words or concepts that relate to it. These details are then written around the main idea to create a web of interrelated concepts.

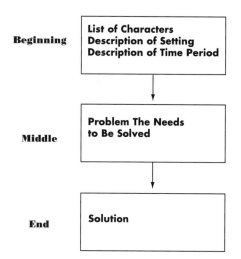

"Sequence maps" help readers gain a better understanding of a story's plot by organizing important developments in chronological order. Before working with sequence maps, students are taught the basics of story structure. They learn that the beginning of the story is for the introduction of characters, their setting, and the time when the action takes place. In the middle of the story, the reader learns that there is a problem for the characters to solve. And at the end, the solution is found. The sequence map allows all these major points to be fully understood.

Teachers appreciate the way that graphic organizational techniques help hone students' thinking skills. They are, essentially, a reading-analysis toolkit, and in that way they can greatly help children with comprehension problems.

They're a big help for beginning writers, too. Organizing your thoughts on paper can be a challenge. Most people just write off the cuff, but graphic organizational tools, such as sequence maps and Venn diagrams have even helped teachers (not to mention other adult professionals) to organize what they want to say and how they say it.

More and more students—the very people for whom these techniques were originally designed to help—are starting to appreciate them, too. In many schools, the use of graphic organizers is so ingrained that when a teacher walks into a classroom it is not at all uncommon for the children to ask "Are we going to use graphic organizers for this?" By now they *know* what these techniques are all about.

It should come as a great relief to parents that teachers, on the whole, are very supportive of the new tests' goals. Most teachers appreciate and respect the ideas behind the tests because they seem to have a genuinely positive and constructive effect on how children think and how they organize what they think. The consensus is that standardized tests for elementary school students are going to change the educational process. Schools are going to turn out children who are able to think on their own, as well as both write and answer comprehensive questions. There is little question that the skills tests wants to "teach" are core, but the pressure that states are putting on schools in every district in the country is intense.

From property values to simple feelings of local pride, we look to our school's for far more than education alone. In effect, what's riding on a school's—or a school district's—scores is our reputation as a community and our standing with the state. Not any less important are the parents' feelings. They, too, look at the statewide scores and ask, "Why weren't we Number One?"

Because of these pressures teachers can't start preparing a month or two before the test and expect students to do well. Consequently, elementary school faculties have begun to devise ways for children to start learning certain skills at the first-grade level, not only in reading, but also in social studies, art, science, and math. Now, even first-graders will be introduced to word webbing and Venn diagrams. Just two years after the new tests began, "teaching for the test" has already trickled down.

WHAT YOU CAN DO

Although it's important to understand grade-level expectations, it is equally important not to get hung up on them. More important still is the fact that every child is different. No one should be expected to conform completely to any norm. The maturity factor, in particular, should never be underestimated. A child whose birthday is later than most of her classmates may be on a slightly later developmental track than her peers. It stands to reason that she will need a little more time—a little more room—in which to develop and mature intellectually.

But, as all of us know, it is so much easier to plan to be patient than it is to actually follow through. Fortunately, there are a few rules of thumb that experienced teachers and parents recommend.

Try the following simple dos and don'ts as you help your child begin to work through his reading difficulties.

Do

Be encouraging
Be positive
Communicate with the teacher
Be a reading role model
Read together
Allow your child time to develop emotionally and
    intellectually
Set a time for reading every day
Make frequent trips to the library or bookstore
Be calm
Be enthusiastic
Listen to your child
Make books accessible on low shelves

Don't

Threaten your child if he can't read to the expected level
Belittle your child's efforts
Express your fears ("If you don't learn to read, you'll never
    get a job")
Compare your child to siblings or others in her class
Pressure or rush your child to take on tasks he is not devel-
    opmentally ready to do
Hide books or make them inaccessible in any other way

Adjusting what we expect from our children's education is not easy, especially in the current political maelstrom, but it is encouraging knowing that so many seasoned teachers and educators are making the best of the situation and offering our children unprecedented opportunities to learn and think. In other words, "teaching to the test?" does not mean "the end of education as we know it!" On the contrary, the classroom experience is becoming more varied and vital than ever before: Children are being offered a range of exciting choices to learn according to their interests and strengths, as well as their emotional and developmental readiness.

Whether your first or second grader is learning to read from an ardent proponent of phonics or an aficionado of whole language, his or her approach will be tempered by state and local guidelines that absolutely insist that every child receive the benefits of a balanced methodology. In all likelihood your child's teacher is offering her the best of both worlds and preparing your child for a rich and rewarding lifetime of learning.

Having said that, however, remember that few influences are more powerful than yours as a parent to affect the process. Stay involved in your child's acquisition of reading skills—the payoff will be incalculable.

3

The Parent-Teacher Meeting

▼

When your child is progressing well in school, a meeting with his teacher is something you hardly need to think about: You just breeze in, listen politely, maybe ask a quick question or two, and off you go. It all seems so routine that some parents don't even make it to the annual Parent-Teacher Night.

A special meeting about your child—whether it was initiated by her classroom teacher or by you—is another story entirely. This is a meeting you *have* to think about, plan for, and take seriously. It's a wonderful opportunity to establish a feeling of teamwork and shared purpose among the important adults in your child's life. It's a chance to get a fresh start on her academic career.

It can also be a little scary.

It's almost impossible not to take your child's reading problem personally. Give yourself time to feel sad, angry, and even guilty, but don't fall into the trap of letting these emotions control your reactions. Recognizing that your child has a problem and accepting it is very difficult. But the sooner you do, the faster the problem can be corrected. Also, remember that you and your child's teacher are on the same side and have the same goal.

●　　●　　●

PREPARING TO MEET

Although it can be a challenge to coordinate the hectic schedules of parents and teachers, meeting early before the school day begins is an excellent option because it takes relatively little time away from work or other family responsibilities. If a potential problem is recognized early in the academic year, a parent-teacher meeting can be arranged by November, with a follow-up meeting in March. A third meeting in May is generally a good idea so that parents and teachers can work together to arrive at an informed consensus regarding the child's next academic year. Of course it is vital to stay in touch between meetings—and, if it is possible, to schedule as many meetings as are needed to help correct reading or other learning problems before they become really serious. Before you meet with your child's teacher, calmly let your child know what's going on. Don't hide the truth from her. Instead, encourage her to talk about the situation, find out if she can think of any issues or details that you should bring up at the meeting. But don't be surprised if she can't. Few first or second grade children are developmentally prepared to be this self-aware. At the same time, your child is sophisticated enough to understand that something isn't quite "right" or that there is a "problem." The last thing you want to do is to make her feel that she has done something bad and is responsible for the circumstances that have led to a meeting with her teacher. Try to be as optimistic and upbeat as you can about discussing the upcoming meeting. Let her know that you are conferring with her teacher because you love her, value her education, and are concerned about making her future as happy and successful as possible.

What to Do Before the Meeting

If you can, arrange the parent-teacher conference at least a week or so in advance. This will give both you and your child's teacher adequate time to prepare for the meeting. It is a very good idea to come in with a list of questions and concerns, such as the ones on page 46. In all likelihood, your child's teacher will have prepared some notes and thoughts about her as well. In fact, real progress can be made, even at your very first meeting, if both of you are willing to share and openly discuss all the issues.

Optimally, both you and your spouse or partner will play a significant role in your child's educational life, so both parents should be at the meeting. Of course, every family has its own realities and schedules—or other factors may make it impossible for both parents to attend. However, from your child's point of view, it is important to see that all the adults in her life care deeply enough about her education and progress to attend this meeting.

Therefore, be sure to make baby-sitting arrangements so that you and your spouse or partner will be able to speak frankly, well out of your child's (or her siblings') hearing. You can and should review the meeting with your child afterwards, but this is not a discussion that she should be part of.

Allow for plenty of time to talk with the teacher; at least half an hour. There may be a number of possible problems to discuss and potential solutions to explore. You don't want to feel rushed.

Also, plan for some time after the meeting to "digest" what has transpired. Perhaps your babysitter can stay for an extra hour so you can go out for coffee and read over your notes from the meeting. The sooner you review what was said, the more easily you'll be able to pinpoint additional questions and decide on your next steps.

Gathering Facts

Your child watches you closely and constantly for clues about the way the world works. Now it's your turn to watch him. Be a private eye for a day and dispassionately observe the way your child's world operates. (Yes, it may be that he becomes "a different child" once he walks through the schoolhouse door; we've all seen how children can display different facets of their personalities in varying situations. But by and large the child you see every day is the child his teacher sees, too.) Concentrate for now on how your child reacts to new things in his environment, how quickly he becomes bored, and what topics hold his interest the longest. Listen carefully as he talks about his day, and notice his body language: his eyes might light up when he talks about an art project, or he may gesticulate in excitement when describing his gym class's activities. Watch him as he moves through the day, early and late, before and after meals. If you aren't present before or after school, enlist the help of your child's caregiver. Then use the worksheet, below, to organize what you've seen.

When you're finished observing, shift gears back into parent mode and read through your notes. You may be surprised to find that the mental picture you have of your child doesn't quite fit with his actual behavior. Or it may become clear that your child is overtired, eating poorly, or not getting enough exercise—problems you can start addressing right away.

But even if the problem can't be solved easily, your observations will help you choose reading materials that will interest and help your child (see Chapter 7), as well as inform your discussions with his teacher and other experts. The better you understand your child's difficulty, the better you can help him find a solution to it.

Worksheet:
A Typical Weekday for My Child

▼

Hours of sleep last night _____

Mood on waking _____

Ate for breakfast: _____

Morning routine: self-starter or needed constant reminding? _____

Mood on leaving for school _____

Ate for lunch: _____

Mood after school _____

Time spent on:

   Homework _____

   Reading (to self or being read to) _____

   Quiet play _____

   Active play _____

   Watching TV _____

   Computer use or video games _____

Ate for dinner: _____

Mood in evening/at bedtime _____

Evening routine: self-starter or needed constant reminding? _____

_____

_____

Think of specific recent incidents to give a one-word description of your child's response in the following situations.

When challenged, my child _____

When frustrated, my child _____

When successful, my child _____

When a request is denied, my child _____

When corrected, my child_____

When disciplined, my child _____

Other observations:_____

_____

_____

_____

WORKING WITH THE TEACHER

When it comes right down to it, teachers appreciate parents who care, so any step you take to help your child learn will be valued. Still, some ways of communicating with your child's teacher are better than others.

First, respect the teacher's knowledge and expertise—even if you disagree with her assessment of, or actions toward, your child. With few exceptions, teachers are highly trained and deeply dedicated individuals. They are faced with myriad responsibilities both within and outside the classroom. "Siding" with your child against his teacher may be tempting, but it will only hurt him in the long run.

Take some time to understand the teacher's classroom routines and teaching philosophy, as well as such school-wide issues such as class size, funding, and test-score pressure. If you want to know more about your child's school, go to www.asd.com. The American School Directory has information pertaining to each of the 108,000 elementary schools in the United States. Chapter 2 outlines some of these issues, but talk with your child and with the teacher herself to learn more about the backdrop against which your child is trying to learn.

What You Should Ask the Teacher

Take some time for yourself in the days before the meeting to give a little thought to what you really need to get from your time with your child's teacher. There are many things you can do to help your child, and you may be harboring fears about what could happen if things don't improve. Don't let your questions and worries fester. Use the meeting to get them out in the open, and then you'll be able to understand the situation with clear eyes and an open mind. Most parents want to know the following things about their child:

> ➤ What is my child doing well at?
> ➤ In what ways do you see him struggling?
> ➤ Does anything in class grab and hold his interest?
> ➤ What would you say his learning style is?
> ➤ How are you engaging him on this level?
> ➤ Will my child have to repeat the grade as a result of this problem?

Cooperating

The meeting with your child's teacher should proceed in an atmosphere of give-and-take. You're on the same side, after all, so treat the teacher as a valued colleague, instead of an unapproachable authority figure or worse, the hired help.

Be prepared to be honest and share sensitive issues with your child's teacher, both during the meeting and throughout your working relationship. It's quite common for a child's schoolwork to suffer if her family is going through any kind of stress—for example, a family illness, an impending divorce, financial worries, or any kind of problem at home. The strain may not show in her outward appearance or mood, but it can have a significant impact on her ability to concentrate and learn. Consequently, she may backslide academically or regress socially. Your child's teacher will be a valuable ally in your efforts to help your child through a difficult time, and you can expect her to keep information about your family confidential, as you would expect any professional to do. No matter how sensitive or mundane the information you share with your child's teacher, it will give her invaluable insights into your child's needs at this time and will undoubtedly have an impact on any plans you make to help your child. So again, be as frank and forthcoming as you possibly can be with your child's teacher. The payoff can be enormous.

Listening

While it's important to consider what you plan to say at your parent-teacher meeting, it's equally important for you to remember to listen. You know your child best, but your child's teacher is the one with the expertise and the experience of having worked with many children. Only together will you be able to make real progress on your child's behalf. So remember to stop talking sometimes, sit back, and open your mind to what the teacher is trying to tell you. Jot down notes, or if the teacher agrees, tape-record the discussion for future reference. If anything is unclear to you, repeat it: "So you're saying that Emma is having a hard time staying focused in class?"

Communicating

Make a point of remaining in touch with the teacher throughout the year to keep her updated on your child's activities and

> **"**An old problem flared up again and was noted on my son George's report card one term. My father had passed away recently, and of course there was a lot going on—I was away from home to be with him during his illness, and it was a very emotional time. George's teacher said she could tell something was on his mind that some regression was going on. It helped when I let her know what was happening, so she could put his behavior in context.**"**
>
> —A MOM IN DELAWARE

progress. It's up to you to write the note, make the phone call, or use whatever mode of communication seems to be most effective for both of you. Remember, the teacher has twenty or thirty children to track; you are the one with the close-up view of just one child, so for practical purposes, take the initiative. In all likelihood your child's teacher will be very glad to meet you halfway.

Some parents also make a point of notifying teachers about less momentous problems that might have an impact on classroom behavior. There's no need to be formal about it. Just take a piece of loose-leaf paper, date it, and state the case: "Robby was stung by a bee yesterday, so he's taking Benadryl today. You might notice that he's a little sleepy." Always include a phone number where you can be reached that day, just in case there are any questions.

In general, the notes you send to the teacher do not have to be formal. Because you are probably just as busy as your child's teacher, it's perfectly acceptable to jot a quick note on a small sheet of notebook paper, or even on the back of an envelope, if you need to communicate an earlier pick-up time than usual or explain your child's absence if he's been out of school for a few days with the flu. The main thing is to stay connected and give your child's teacher the message that you are the other half of a viable partnership.

At the same time, don't hesitate to take full advantage of new communication technologies, if they're offered to you. Many teachers are now giving out their e-mail addresses and inviting parents to contact them that way. Some schools even have a web page where teachers write little blurbs or post pictures that show what their classes have been learning.

On the other hand, ongoing, casual face-to-face contact with your child's teacher is a great way to stay in touch, if your schedule allows it. For example, if you volunteer in your child's class, you can get a firsthand look at how the teacher relates to the students and see what your child is working on. You can also get a much better sense of how the school day progresses, which, in turn, gives you a better idea of what to talk to your child about when he comes home. Even if it's just for one morning a month, volunteering is a great way to keep up-to-date on your child's progress—both social and academic—as well as observe how he interacts with his teacher, classmates, and friends. If you're in the classroom helping, the teacher will get to know you and keep you informed in person—which can be a great advantage.

While all of these methods are helpful, nothing can replace a formal meeting between you and the teacher for a focused conversation about your child's potential, progress, and problems. One parent-teacher conference may be all you need to get things going, so try to meet one-on-one with the teacher in the early stages of your reading-improvement project.

One thing to avoid is sending verbal messages to school via your child. Like a game of "Telephone," the ideas can easily be garbled. And putting your child in the middle of any kind of exchange between adults is hardly fair.

Arts and Letters

There's an art to writing an effective note to your child's teacher. It should be short and to the point, but not unfriendly. Nor should it be flip or jokingly casual, as your child's education is serious business.

The following letter contains elements that teachers appreciate most in notes from parents: it's friendly, polite, provides useful information, asks pertinent questions, includes phone numbers and times to call, and everything is properly spelled.

November 27, 2000

Dear Mrs./Mr./Ms. _____,

I hope you enjoyed the long weekend. I'm just writing to let you know that I've been a bit concerned about Nicholas's language arts homework over the last two weeks or so. He seems to be taking longer than usual to finish his work, and is less interested in correcting mistakes that I bring to his attention.

Have you noticed any changes in his behavior or demeanor lately? Do you think he's been struggling more than usual with the last few reading topics? I'd like to get to the bottom of this before it becomes something serious.

Please feel free to call me at your convenience if you have any thoughts or ideas. I can be reached during the day at my office at 555-1234, or in the evening at 555-5678 until about 10:00.

Thank you in advance for your insights.

Sincerely yours,

• • •

HOW YOU MAY FEEL

Going into your meeting you may know what the issues are and feel well prepared with questions and suggestions of your own, but even so, it's difficult to keep your cool or be objective when the subject in question is so close to your heart. It's completely understandable that your emotions may get the best of you while you're talking about your child.

Don't worry—teachers have seen it all before. Some honest emotion isn't something they can't handle. Remember, too, that many teachers are parents just like you, and their children are not immune to learning problems. Your child's teacher may well have been in your shoes at some point. She can really empathize with your feelings.

If you find yourself getting defensive or angry during the meeting, try to keep things in perspective. The teacher is not out to attack your child. If he points out a weakness, it's because he hopes to work on it *with you* to correct the problem.

Nor is the teacher calling your parenting skills into question. He knows very well that reading problems can be caused by many different factors; he is not blaming you. You may have done everything "right" from birth through first grade—read to your child, talked with your child, spent one-on-one time together—and still there can be a problem. Even so, the situation may dredge up deep-rooted fears, insecurities, and feelings of guilt. Don't be embarrassed if they surface during your meeting. Take a good, deep breath and try to work through them.

If you can, open the meeting with an honest review of what you've noticed about how your child relates to reading and to school, and share whatever reading routines you've tried at home. Let the teacher know if you have any guesses about or insights into the cause of your child's problem.

If you're feeling nervous about the meeting as it approaches, try a role-playing exercise beforehand. Ask your spouse or partner, or a good friend, to take the part of your child's teacher. Then run through all the things you plan to say—your observations, your questions, and your worries. In a mock meeting, the "teacher" won't be able to respond to all these things, but at least you'll have a chance to practice.

> "Being a working mom, I went through some guilt—'Am I not doing enough?' I finally had to realize that I couldn't be everything. We needed some outside help for my daughter's reading problem."
>
> —A MOM IN NEW YORK

•   •   •

MEETING CHECKLIST

Before

❑ Plan the meeting

❑ Make baby-sitting arrangements

❑ Make observations of my child

❑ Consider the family schedule and home dynamic

❑ Make list of questions

During

❑ Ask all questions on list

❑ Get answers to every question

❑ Make joint plan of action

❑ Establish good working relationship with teacher

❑ Understand what teacher will do for my child

❑ Understand what teacher expects of me

❑ Set a re-evaluation date

After

❑ Set aside reading time every day

❑ Get assessments as needed

❑ Buy learning materials as needed

❑ Hire tutor or other help as needed

❑ Stay in regular contact with teacher

MAKING AN ACTION PLAN

The goal of the meeting is not to solve your child's problem right then and there, but to devise a solid plan of attack. Whether it's a phonics program, flash-card drills, time management, a health evaluation, or formal tutoring, your child's teacher will always try to give you suggestions about how to achieve both immediate and

66 "When "self-con-
trol problems" came
home on John's
report card, we just
gasped, "At school
too!" because he's
the same way at
home. I resolved to
meet with the
teacher right away.
At our conference
she described her
take on the problem,
and I assured her
that what John was
doing in school was
not acceptable
behavior at home,
either. In the end,
she worked with him
and *we* worked with
him to encourage
John to think more
about other people's
feelings. I walked
away from the expe-
rience feeling really
good about it. 99

—A MOM IN
DELAWARE

long term goals, while factoring in how time and financial resources might affect the equation. It is very important to reinforce and follow through *at home* on the suggestions your child's teacher has made. However, if parents encounter problems they should not hesitate to re-open the conversation with the teacher.

Getting an Outside Opinion

Your action plan may need some form of outside review if you come to the conclusion that your child may be experiencing vision, hearing, perception, or other physical problems. If so, be sure to keep the teacher informed of any diagnosis and keep her up-to-date on your child's therapy.

Keep this in mind for *next* September, too—your child's new teacher should be informed of the past problem and any continuing efforts to deal with it: You don't want to start the whole process all over again with each new teacher. For example, if your child is being treated for a visual-perceptual problem, make a point of telling the teacher about it on the first day of school. All it takes is a short note that says something as simple as, "My daughter is being tutored for a visual-perceptual problem, please be aware that she should sit in the front of the classroom," and so on. The teacher will be glad you told her about your child's special circumstances because very often this kind of information is not communicated from grade to grade. As a parent, you should never assume that it is.

Evaluating Your Action Plan

Before you leave the first parent-teacher meeting, be sure to set up another time to review and evaluate your action plan. Working toward a firm goal will help all of you stay focused. A less formal, ongoing kind of evaluation—a "let's-stay-in-touch" kind of agreement—might feel comfortably casual, but your child will not benefit if you don't follow up on it diligently.

You might want to keep a log or journal of the steps and techniques you are trying at home: Note what works and doesn't work for your child, and jot down your observations of the improvements she makes. These notes will make it easy to compose regular updates for the teacher, and will help you make ongoing assessments of your child's progress.

Don't forget to ask the teacher to tell you which milestones and signs of progress you should be watching out for. These will vary depending on your child's situation, but might include the ability to read a certain level of book, the quick recognition of all letters and letter sounds, or a willingness to venture a prediction about a story's outcome.

And don't be surprised if you have to change tactics at a moment's notice. Try to be as flexible and receptive as possible to changes in the plan: Children change. If you or the teacher feels that a different course of action would be beneficial, keep an open mind.

ASSESSING YOUR CHILD'S SKILLS

Many schools and school districts have a system in place for sharing information and possible solutions to students' school-related problems. In-school assessment teams may include various teachers, remedial specialists, health professionals, and administrators who gather to discuss a child's difficulties, review possible solutions, and support the child's classroom teacher.

However, some parents prefer to rely on their own experts, professionals who can meet with, test, and evaluate their child. In addition, there are a number of tests—published in book form or accessible over the Internet—that can help you identify and deal with your child's learning problem. For more information on formal assessment, please see Chapter 7, "When You Need Expert Help."

Finally, keep in mind that your child's current learning difficulties don't have to define his future. Most schools really are set up to serve and support children. Nevertheless, make it your responsibility to stay on top of your child's education. No matter how "good" her teacher is she can't possibly know your child as well as you do, especially these days, when the average elementary school class contains thirty to thirty-five students. If you or her teacher becomes aware of a change in your child's attitude toward school, or if she is falling behind in some way, do not waste a moment to investigate the circumstances.

Early diagnosis of a learning problem is half the battle, and few diagnostic tools are more useful than periodic parent-teacher meetings. Once you know there's a problem, you can enlist the help not only of your child's teacher and experienced school teams, but outside professionals as well. The key is to stick with your action plan, even if it changes from time to time, and to continue the dialogue with your child's teacher. Think of him as your most important ally in the campaign to help your child progress and enjoy school.

4

Homework

Seeing your child off to school, especially if he is in the first or second grade, is a truly moving experience for most parents. There are so many mixed emotions: joy, excitement, expectation—and yes, a little worry, too. After years of orchestrating your child's day it can feel strange to let him go, to be separated from him for several hours without knowing exactly what he's doing, or if his needs—both emotional and educational—are being met. And, as most parents know, it can be tricky to get a clear sense of what is going on in the classroom from your six or seven year old. He may be learning how to read, write, add and subtract, but in all likelihood his mind will be preoccupied with more immediate interests when he gets home, especially the first hour or two, when most children need a little down time to digest the day's events. The temptation to quiz your child about what he's doing in school may be strong, but try to resist and give him room to relax and enjoy a little unstructured time.

Ideally, a child's transition from play and relaxation to doing homework should be as smooth as possible. Most children like to participate in the decision regarding when and where they will do their homework. Involving your child in this kind of decision both encourages him to think on his own and gives him the message that his judgment is valued. After all, one of the most important objectives of your child's education is to help him become an independent thinker and learner. At the same time you want to be a responsible parent and encourage sound work habits that will support what he is learning in school. This is exactly what your child's teacher would like to see as well. Indeed, most education professionals agree that homework plays an essential role in reinforcing the concepts a child has practiced in school. Many teachers envision homework as a form of closure to the day's curriculum—an important step in gently but actively cementing the main idea of a lesson. In order to support the efforts of your child's teacher, you'll want to reinforce the idea that homework is just as important to the learning process as schoolwork. Fortunately, there's a lot you can do to help make your child's first- and second-grade homework experiences positive and successful.

Setting the Mood

Just as we're most comfortable sleeping in the bedroom and working in the office, children do homework best in settings that feel right for them. Create a "homework zone" that will help your child work comfortably and well.

- Turn off the TV, radio, CD player, and anything else that might create a visual or audible distraction.
- Reserve a special work space for your child, or if that's not possible, clear a table with enough room for all of his books, papers, and supplies.
- A regular "homework spot" is helpful for most children, even if the area is used for other purposes at different times of the day (the kitchen or dining room table, for example).
- Make sure your child is comfortable. (She might feel more at ease changing out of "school clothes," or even just shedding her socks and shoes.)
- Encourage younger siblings (and pets) to play elsewhere.
- Make reference materials easily accessible.
- Be available for consultations—if not yourself, then a "homework helper" or another member of the family.

THE LOGIC BEHIND HOMEWORK

Many teachers believe that first and second graders should spend at least a half-hour and perhaps as much as an hour each day on homework, although there is some difference of opinion. For example, some professionals firmly believe that homework is most effective for first and second graders when it does not exceed twenty minutes. If you are concerned about the length of time your child spends on homework, discuss the matter with his teacher. In all likelihood he will be more than happy to explain his reasons for assigning a certain amount of time each night for homework. Understanding the educational process and methods behind homework assignments will help both you and your child establish a consistent homework routine that *feels right*.

In any case, many teachers believe the time spent doing homework should include some review of the day's learning, as well as work on daily assignments and long-term projects.

THE IMPORTANCE OF DAILY REVIEW

Educators of every stripe agree that first and second grade are the foundation of a child's entire educational career. Every concept taught in these crucial years is designed to form the matrix on which his future learning can grow. This is why a review component should be a regular part of your child's homework routine: the skills she learns now need to be well absorbed in order for her intellect to grow.

While your child is doing her homework, be sure to offer your support and encouragement. After she has completed her work, be sure to review it for accuracy and neatness. One way to review is simply to sit down with your child and go over the evening's homework assignments together, line by line. Ask questions about both right and wrong answers alike "How did you come up with that answer?" "Where in the story does it say that?" "Can you think of other words with that vowel sound?" Having to answer questions in different ways will help your child fix the concepts in her mind as well as reinforce other aspects of the assignment.

Of course the review process is an excellent way of ascertaining whether or not your child has understood the assignment, but there are a number of other reasons why it is important:

➤ It shows that you are actively involved in your child's education and that you take both her and her work seriously.

➤ It helps your child understand that she is responsible for the work she does.

➤ It ensures that your child understands your expectations
for homework.
➤ It underscores the importance of completing work.

REGULAR ASSIGNMENTS FOR FIRST GRADERS

A typical example of reading homework for first graders is a
review of what the teacher taught that day from the basal reader,
which is how teachers often refer to a reading textbook. For
example, if the reading lesson focused on the long A combinations
"ai" and "ay," homework that night might include a page from
the skills book. This gives children a chance to practice the sound
combinations they learned during the day, on new words. On days
when new vocabulary words and a new story are introduced,
homework might involve writing and using the words to create
sentences and re-reading the story to a parent that night.

Some first-grade homework assignments might look like these:

Monday night: Write two sentences in your "Reading
Journal" about the book we are reading in class.
Tuesday night: Read the handout I gave to you in class
today and draw a picture of the main character.
Wednesday night: Write each of the spelling words once in
your spelling notebook.
Thursday night: Write five words that begin with the letter
"t."

REGULAR ASSIGNMENTS FOR SECOND GRADERS

Some second-grade teachers give their students a set homework
routine to follow each week throughout the school year. Every
night they give their students homework in math and spelling, two
important subjects that require daily reinforcement. At the beginning of the year, each child in the class is given a schedule that outlines the class's weekly spelling routine. For example, it might read:

Monday night: Write all your spelling words three times
each.

Tuesday night: Put your spelling words in ABC order.

Wednesday night: Write a sentence for each of your spelling words—that's four sentences.

Thursday night: Study and practice for the spelling test tomorrow (Friday).

A schedule such as the one above is important for children on the second-grade level because it gives them a feeling of security that comes with knowing what to expect.

OTHER HOMEWORK OPTIONS

Some teachers prefer to give their students more variety in homework assignments. To give their students some sense of predictability, however, they may hand out a new page of homework assignments at the beginning of each week. Assignments may include:

➤ Workbook pages
➤ Word searches and five minutes of reading
➤ Write-your-own math problems
➤ "Cloze" activities (fill in the blank)
➤ Fifteen to twenty minutes of writing in a journal
➤ Reading a book to a parent or older sibling for fifteen minutes over the weekend

Still other teachers vary the homework from day to day, but consistently assign twenty to thirty minutes of homework each night. These teachers usually post the daily assignment on the blackboard and ask the students to copy it down in their notebooks. Before dismissal, some teachers ask to hear their students' version of the assignment just to be extra sure that they understand it.

However the assignment is made, teachers at this level agree that a consistent routine is important for students, teachers, and parents alike. Be sure you understand how your child's homework is assigned and how his teacher expects it to be completed.

As the school year progresses, your child's teacher will expect him to take more responsibility for his homework. He should be able to read independently and understand directions by the end of first grade. You should be able to step back from the process and become involved only to help solve a problem, or to assist with planning and organizing special projects. Nevertheless, don't forget to give your child the sense that you *are available*—whenever he needs you—to share the adventure of learning something new.

Special Projects

Special homework projects run the gamut from book reports to poster board displays. Special projects may require students to conduct some form of research and express themselves through writing or art.

Projects are a favorite assignment among teachers for the multi-faceted learning experiences they provide. The best of them foster children's reading skills while encouraging them to organize their ideas, and present them in a variety of creative—and sometimes artistically expressive—ways. Children love almost any hands-on approach to learning and enjoy working with a variety of materials. For most students a special project provides a refreshing break from standard texts and the usual classroom routines, while giving them the precious opportunity to explore a favorite—or new—subject in his or her own way. Parents, on the other hand, often dread special projects—especially if their children have a tendency to put them off until the night before they are due. When this happens it is very hard to resist the temptation to help your child. But, as with any other homework assignment, there is really no value whatsoever in having the work done by anybody but the student. Instead, help your child plan his work, and then help him stick to those plans. If he has a book report to do, for example, encourage him to do a little bit every day, so that he doesn't have to do everything at the last minute. Children at this age legitimately *do* need guidance when it comes to setting up a special project, deciding on the kind of work that's required, and sticking to a reasonable schedule. There is no question that your enthusiasm and support are invaluable to your child's efforts, but try to be as firm as you can be about whose responsibility it is, ultimately, to *do* the project.

WORK SPACES AND ROUTINES

Whatever kind of work you do, you wouldn't dream of doing it without the proper tools. In the same way, a student needs the right atmosphere and the right equipment to approach her home work in an organized, disciplined, and thoughtful way. For most children, routine is a key factor in making homework a normal, expected, scheduled event in their day. Find a spot somewhere in your home that would be just right for your child's Homework Zone. A child-size desk or table is great, but not necessary. A coffee table, kitchen bar, or even the dining room table can work just as well. No matter where it is, make sure your child's Homework Zone is well lit, with a desk lamp or another good source of light. Also, make sure that the seating is comfortable for your child. (It's hard to concentrate when you can't see what you're doing or feel that your chair is the wrong size.) Finding the right location, however, is very important: At this age, most children's homework needs to be pretty closely supervised, so you may want her to be close to a family room or kitchen, wherever an adult might be nearby.

Make sure the space you choose is cleared of the ordinary clutter of family life before homework time begins. If junk mail, forgotten toys, or newspapers pile up there, it may distract your child. If there is only one neat spot in your home, let it be your child's Homework Zone.

SUPPLIES

Your child's special zone needs supplies—and lots of them. For one thing, children love an array of quirky pencils, magic markers, bubble-gum pink erasers and their own pencil box, complete with secret compartments and favorite pens. For many children, having these special "tools" on hand seems to make doing homework assignments a lot more fun. So be sure that your child has plenty of them within easy reach. Some children have a tendency to postpone homework, and might even turn the search for a sharpened pencil into an exciting twenty-minute detour, but you can help bring your child back to the task at hand with a drawer or box full of special "for-homework-use-only" supplies. You might even sweeten the deal by occasionally surprising your child with a goofy new eraser, a packet of brightly colored construction paper, or an extra-long pencil. Sometimes writing the week's spelling words over and over is a lot more interesting if you have a new pencil on hand.

For the Gallo family, homework supplies—glue, a ruler, different colored pencils, highlighters, crayons, and tape—are kept in "the green box." When George, the Gallo's seven-year-old, needs anything for an assignment his mother gets out "the green box." George even lets his little brother Michael use the materials, but only when the box is already out for homework. And when they're done with the work, everything goes back in the box.

Here's a list of supplies that your child will most likely need:

- ➤ Sharpened pencils
- ➤ Pencil sharpener
- ➤ Pens
- ➤ Writing paper
- ➤ Eraser
- ➤ Box of crayons
- ➤ Magic Markers
- ➤ Ruler
- ➤ Tape
- ➤ Scissors
- ➤ Glue stick
- ➤ Scrap paper
- ➤ Construction paper
- ➤ Hole punch
- ➤ Stapler

REFERENCE MATERIALS

Reference books, such as a children's dictionary and encyclopedia should also be handy. Your child will be learning research skills during these years, so encourage her to look up anything she doesn't know. Fortunately, there are many children's reference books available, and she may be able to use them by herself. If she needs to use an adult dictionary, atlas, or encyclopedia, be sure to give her a hand. Knowing how to make use of reference materials is an important habit to develop early in a child's academic career. Be sure she can find these materials easily.

Other Sources of Information

You may want to make a computer accessible for reference purposes as well. Many encyclopedias are available online and on CD, and of course Internet search engines can dredge up tons of sites relating to any keyword. However, computer use at this age does need to be closely supervised. Spend some time with any reference CD before giving your child free access to it, and be at his side whenever he does online research. It's all too easy for a child to wander into inappropriate or unsavory Internet territory.

Television Pros and Cons

TV is almost inevitably a force in your child's life—whether yours is a household of dedicated channel surfers or PBS-only viewers. Our culture is so attuned to the medium that it is almost impossible to avoid it.

Without a doubt, excess TV viewing exerts a negative influence on a child, leading him away from active efforts, imaginative play, and reading. Some parents whose children are struggling in school find that a severe cutback in TV time is a first step toward a new, more academically oriented life. As one Dad put it, "Sometimes you just have to discourage the mindless hours in front of the TV, or even the computer screen. We bombard children with so many influences and stimuli that make them wonder, "Why read? Why write? Why bother?' "

So it makes sense to take a critical look at your child's relationship with TV. Think about how many hours a day he watches, why he's watching rather than doing something else, and perhaps most importantly, what it is he's watching.

On the positive side, children's television is, in some ways, in the midst of a golden age, with more and better programming choices than ever before. The production values, writing quality, and imaginative content of children's shows have vastly improved over the last few years. New federal laws that mandate the networks to broadcast "educational" fare can be credited for this sea change, or you can chalk it up to the fact that advertisers are seeing more profit in appealing to children. Either way, the effect is real.

However, this doesn't mean you can just let your children loose with a remote and a bag of chips every day after school. You're the parent, and it's up to you to help your children make smart choices about what they watch on television. Look for shows that:

- Emphasize reading reinforcement and phonics review. "Between the Lions" (PBS) is a fabulous half-hour of songs, stories, and silliness set in a library that's run by a family of lions. Each episode hinges on a particular vowel sound (short o is honored by a retelling of the "Pandora's Box" story, for example) and features celebrity walk-ons, running gags, and decoding exercises disguised as funny skits.

- Explore a particular subject area in an engaging way. Fox's "The Magic School Bus" based on the popular book series, sends a class of children hurtling through time and space with their amazing teacher, Ms. Frizzle, to learn about science and nature from rather unusual angles—like inside a classmate's digestive system.

- Present problem-solving story lines. One of the main preoccupations of children this age is getting along with peers and family. "Dragon Tales" uses elements of both fantasy and reality to tell simple stories of challenge, failure, re-trying, and success that really resonate with young children. That the main characters include siblings, friends, and a teacher figure—some of whom are, in fact, dragons—makes the show all the more appealing.

- Tell stories from literature. The Disney Channel's "Madeline" and PBS's "Wishbone" are shows based on books that draw viewers towards reading the originals.

- Put a positive spin on reading. "Arthur" (PBS), which is wildly popular among six and seven year olds for its realistic schoolyard dramas (albeit populated by anthropomorphic aardvarks, rabbits, and monkeys), frequently sets stories and even musical sequences in the local library.

- "Reading Rainbow" is probably one of the best shows to foster your child's interest in reading. In every episode children suggest and review books they have read and enjoyed. Host LeVar Burton shows children a world where books are magic. You can also visit the website at http://gpn.unl.edu/rainbow

You might want to steer your children away from shows that exist only to promote a product. Positive values may be included, but the value of advertising is usually paramount in shows like these. Also to be avoided are programs that talk down to children, and which don't challenge their intellects, tastes, or emotions.

Above all, try to sit down with your child and watch TV with him whenever you can. Talk about what you're seeing: "What's another way Arthur could solve this problem?" "How do you think the kids felt when Ms. Frizzle sent the bus up that kid's nose?" Talk about the commercials, too, and help your child learn smart consumer skills.

GETTING A LITTLE PEACE AND QUIET

Although a cathedral silence need not descend the moment homework begins, the Homework Zone should be relatively quiet. Of course, there are children who learn better in the presence of some kinds of background noise, such as music. Nevertheless all family members should participate, to the extent that they can, in maintaining a calm atmosphere while the student does her work. You might begin with turning off the TV—probably the single most distracting element in any home. Turn down or turn off radios, CDs, or tapes. Let the answering machine pick up the calls. Encourage younger siblings to stay occupied with books, coloring, or quiet play. Above all, be available for your child if any sort of consultation is needed, or ask another adult to stand in for you. An adult presence also helps to keep your child's attention focused on her work.

ESTABLISHING A ROUTINE
THAT WORKS FOR YOUR CHILD

For most children a set pattern for doing homework is enormously helpful. And for some, it is the only way homework gets done at all. The goal is to make doing homework into a good habit— one of those incontestable things that children just *do* on a daily basis—like brushing their teeth or getting regular exercise.

Every family eventually establishes a workable homework routine, whether it involves having a snack first and then quiet time for work—or the other way around. Some families encourage physical exercise of one kind or another before homework begins, while others simply endorse a rule-free hour of "down time." Whatever pattern you establish, the keys to making it work are regularity and consistency. In other words, establishing a routine for your child is the most effective way of demonstrating that homework is a normal, expected, everyday, and very important activity.

Every child is different of course, so the routine you establish for your first grader may be very different from some of her classmates'. You may be more relaxed, for example, about exactly when your child does her homework every day, as long as it takes place within an accepted range of time. Or you might be more flexible about the occasional play date—an activity that most first and second graders absolutely adore—even if it throws off your child's usual homework schedule by an hour or two. This will not "hurt" her in the least if she maintains her established homework routine most of the time. On the other hand, an attitude toward homework that is too relaxed usually gives a child the impression that there might be a way of avoiding it. After all, if it's clear that you don't think it's important to do homework either regularly or in a timely fashion, why should your child?

Parents who are away from home during the after-school hours have even more reason to establish a firm routine. Whether a babysitter, family friend, relative, or nanny looks after your child, make it clear that you expect your child to do his homework at a given time. A schedule or chart that assigns specific tasks to set times can be extremely helpful for both your child and his caregiver. Young children really do need structure, and there's nothing like a reliable routine to help give them a sense of direction and accomplishment.

HOMEWORK HELP

According to many teachers who work with first and second graders, parents need to be intimately involved in the homework process at this age. Sitting with your child as he does his homework, gives you a wonderful opportunity to help him when he makes mistakes. If you let the moment go, however, and expect his teacher to correct his errors, your child may miss a valuable learning opportunity altogether. The reason is that many elementary school teachers simply don't have the time to go over every night's homework assignment with each child. Classroom size can be

> "Usually, I encourage my boys do their homework as soon as they walk in the door—before they play outside or watch TV. I answer the door and the phone to shoo away their friends until the homework's done. I've discovered that whenever I let them put off their homework, the boys end up with forgotten assignments, work that is done too quickly, or takes too long. Putting it off is just too disruptive all the way around."
>
> —THE MOM OF A FIRST AND SECOND GRADER

staggeringly high in some schools, which contributes to the limited amount of time teachers can spend with individual students. If your child has struggled with a homework assignment or has made the same mistake repeatedly, don't hesitate to contact his teacher about it. Even a short, informal note will do: "We had to do this assignment several times because it was so difficult to 'get.' What are we doing wrong?"

At the same time, it's critical that your child does the work himself, or else the value of the homework—its power to fix a concept in your child's memory—will be lost. You certainly don't want to hobble your child's potential for learning by doing his schoolwork for him. At the same time, most teachers recognize a departure from a student's usual style of expression and will know when he hasn't done the work himself. Invariably, this leads to embarrassment on all sides, not to mention the damage it does to a child's confidence in his ability to learn anything on his own.

Of course, getting overly involved in your child's homework is completely understandable. You want her to succeed and do well. And sometimes there's just doesn't seem to be enough time in the day for your child to arrive at the correct answer herself. When time is short and the whole family is rushed, as is so often the case today, parents sometimes end up saying, "Okay, here's the answer, write it down and you're done." Every parent has "been there" at least once, but it is vital to resist the temptation to *speed* up the process of your child's education by giving her the answers! To strike that delicate balance between getting it right and getting it done, cast yourself in the role of your child's homework checker, not his homework collaborator. For example, if you note that your child has made a mistake, don't hesitate to point it out gently. You can bring the error to his attention by saying something along these lines: "You might want to go back over number one" or "Maybe you should check the way this word is spelled." Just give him hints and pointers, but don't make the correction yourself; if necessary, guide your child to the reference or resource that can reveal an answer. This process doesn't have to turn into drudgery. In fact it can be gratifying for both of you, especially if you can make "researching" an answer into a fun, sharing, and productive experience. At the end of the day, the lesson *you'll* have taught your child is that the process of learning almost anything can be immensely satisfying if you have a positive attitude.

TROUBLESHOOTING:
WHEN (AND HOW) TO HELP

Homework problems vary from child to child and home to home, as you might expect, but most of them boil down to the same conflicts. Here are some suggestions for smoothing over some of the most common homework complaints:

"I don't have time."

Prime homework time is in the afternoon, when lessons are still fresh and children are more alert. If your family's schedule is such that a parent isn't present to supervise an afternoon homework session, you're facing a distinct challenge. Getting homework done in a timely fashion is very tough, especially for two-career families. Some parents simply can't get home until 6:00 or later. At that point there isn't much time left in the day to find out about what happened at school, sort through mail, read notices from school, make dinner, and fit in bath time. All this, and homework needs to be done before 7:30 or 8:00 when some children are totally *finished* for the day. This is a tall order to deliver in almost no time at all, especially when Mom and Dad are a bit frazzled themselves. However, there are some things you can do to help reduce the stress of trying to do to many things at the same time in too little time, as well as give your child the affection and attention he needs:

➤ Encourage your child to do his homework in the kitchen while you're preparing dinner. It's not the most peaceful place in the house, but it is where you can supervise him. At this age his homework should take about a half-hour, the same amount of time it takes to prepare a meal.

➤ Set your alarm clock a bit earlier (if you happen to be a family of "morning people") and sit down with your child to do her homework *before* school, rather than trying to squeeze it in at night. One drawback to doing homework in the morning is that the lesson on which the homework is based will be less fresh in your child's mind, and might therefore be a bit more difficult to complete. Still, it's better than keeping her up and working at 10:00 P.M. If a sunrise homework session works for your child, that's what matters. But do be sure that the early wake-up call is not cutting into your child's necessary sleep time. Rest is a major element in school success.

➤ Enlist the help of a relative or hire a babysitter. No matter who your caregiver is, consistency is the key to your child's success with homework. Have a very specific understanding of what the caregiver will ask of your child, and when. Be equally specific with your child about what you expect of her. A task chart is a good way to keep her focused: when she completes the work she can put a sticker on the chart for the day. When you get home, make it your first priority to review the homework with your child. Show her that homework is as important a part of your schedule as you want it to be in hers.

➤ Hire a "homework helper." You might be able to find a high-school student or college undergraduate who is willing to do his homework at your house and supervise your children while they do their own. The helper's job is to make sure that all the written homework and even some studying is done before the parents walk through the door. Another plus: homework helpers charge far less than most tutors—probably about the same as the average teenage babysitter. (See Chapter 8 for more information about hiring a tutor.)

"She works so slowly; homework takes forever."

Typically, first- and second grade teachers expect their students to take about a half-hour to complete homework assignments, although fifteen to forty-five minutes is within the "normal" scheduling range. Any extra time a child takes beyond that, however, usually means that something is going wrong. Here are some of the possibilities:

➤ **Procrastination, or poor time management skills.** If homework is taking longer than it should, find out why. It may be that the child does not understand the instructions and is afraid to ask someone to explain them. Although they may understand the assignment, children will often find ways to waste time before beginning an assignment. They will not have all of the necessary materials with them, or they will find other needs, the need to have a drink of water, or the need to have a snack beforehand to interrupt their work. Children need to learn the value of completing assignments in a timely manner. If there is more than one assignment for homework, help your child plan the homework hour so that harder assignments are completed first, and easier assignments are done last, when your child is most likely to be tired.

➤ **Lack of focus.** Some children may have no problem beginning an assignment, but struggle to see it through to the end. They become distracted and the assignment becomes a task to avoid. Checklists can help a child stay focused on her work. If the homework is broken into different parts, your child can go about it as several smaller assignments. They can focus on these smaller tasks as they complete their homework. Other children are motivated to complete homework assignments within a set time if they are given stickers to put on a special chart. Perhaps you want your child to estimate how long they think an assignment might take. You can set a timer and if they complete the work early, make a note of it in their homework folder, or acknowledge it with a gold star. They will work to complete their assignment in that time, which gives children who have a hard time focusing the ability to stay on track.

"Some nights are fine, but other times she really struggles with her homework."

First, try to discern if there's a pattern to your child's homework problem. Perhaps just one skill or subject area is the source of the trouble. If she can write her spelling words out correctly but gets bogged down in trying to write sentences, try a different approach to the assignment. Set up an achievement chart just for successful sentence completion or suggest that she tackle that subject when you can be available to work closely with her. This does not mean you should do the work for her, but it is certainly appropriate for you to clarify instructions and suggest different ways to complete the assignment. Finishing the assignment will be a success that you can both enjoy.

If you can't trace your child's learning difficulty to a certain type of assignment, other factors may be at work. A social problem, like bullying can have a powerful effect on your child's ability to concentrate. If you suspect this is the case, leave the homework to the side temporarily, sit down with your child, and ask her calmly if she's feeling unwell or in any kind of trouble. Track her eating and sleeping patterns for a week or so and see if you can link them to her difficulties with homework. You may need to involve your child's pediatrician if you suspect a physical cause.

"He just doesn't get it."

Sometimes, homework takes a long time to complete because a child genuinely doesn't understand the concept before him. It's hard to watch your child struggle with anything, homework included. How you react to his frustration is an important factor.

On the whole, it's best to let your child wrestle with assignments himself. Remember that the subject at hand *has* been taught in class, and that the whole point of homework is to reinforce the day's lesson. You do your child no favors by doing the work for him. Guide him toward the correct answer with hints and clues, as discussed earlier in this chapter.

If your child genuinely does not understand his homework, an attempt should be made by you to help him understand the assignment. If you also do not understand what is expected, don't be discouraged. The homework your first or second grader receives is based on what has been completed in the class. You are not expected to know what or how the material was originally presented that day. If you aren't able to determine how to complete the assignment, now is the time to write a quick note to the teacher. Briefly explain the trouble your child is running into. It's certainly possible that the lesson in question was rushed, or that the concept was taught in a way that made it difficult for your child to grasp. Whatever the reason, the classroom teacher should be told when a lesson doesn't "stick." If she hears from you that there was a problem, she's likely to go over the idea again, but from a different angle the next day. Expect to see the same assignment the following night. The teacher is certainly going to be interested to know if your child has grasped the concept the next day.

"He won't pay attention; he just won't do it."

There are so many attractive distractions competing for your child's attention. Why should he keep his mind on homework when the TV and video games are all at his fingertips? Fortunately, there is a wide selection of computer games that are entertaining and educational. Your child's love of computers and video games can be an asset. Instead of purchasing the newest video game, do a little research into the best learning games for children. There are hundreds of quality educational games that your child—believe it or not—will enjoy playing. If this doesn't interest him, set ground rules for video game playing, no games until all homework is complete. Make it a rule and stick to it.

A firm routine for homework time—no ifs, ands, buts, or lat-ers—can work wonders. But the emphasis is on "firm." It doesn't much matter exactly when or where homework is done each day as long as the place and time are consistent. And any fudging of the rules must carry immediate and relevant consequences (tem-porary removal of TV privileges for switching on the set before homework is done, for example).

"After a long school day my child just can't sit another hour."

High-energy children may need some variation in the standard homework routine. A child who's antsy after a day in the class-room deserves a chance to shake off that jumpy feeling. He may need to have his snack before homework time begins. Or you might try putting him through an active drill, like Spelling Cheer (see Chapter 6), before settling down to the assigned work. As long as he attends to his work when the time comes, it's perfectly reasonable to adapt the schedule to the child, rather than the other way around.

"She doesn't have the self-confidence to do it alone."

A child who lacks confidence in her ability to do schoolwork is a prime candidate for tutoring. One-on-one work with a tutor can be a huge confidence booster, especially if the tutor constructs lessons that build success upon success. (See Chapter 8 for more on the tutoring relationship.)

You can help foster your child's self-esteem by focusing on the positive when you check homework together. First, praise your child for the questions she got right, and then offer gentle critiques and hints on how to arrive at the correct answers for questions she missed. Encourage your child's other activities, too—a well-placed "I knew you could do it!" can make a very big difference.

"He keeps forgetting his books."

One of the major lessons of first and second grade is personal responsibility. Your child is supposed to be learning that it's not his parent's job to keep his books and papers straight; it's his. The best way to teach a child to be responsible for his things is to teach him to be organized and prepared by having everything with him. Your child should have a backpack, or other type of book bag in which all of his school supplies are neatly kept. Your child shouldn't leave his school things lying around the house after he has completed his homework. Teach him to replace everything in his backpack. Likewise, homework can be neatly stored in a notebook. Your child will learn to take care of his things and to be responsible for them. If your child does better with a checklist, tape one to his bedroom door, or on his desk at school. As he is going to and from school, it will be his responsibility to go over his checklists to make certain he has his books, homework, and supplies with him. These lessons are important to teach in these formative years. Remember, in first and second grade your child is learning how to be a student. Encourage good habits now and if he happens to forget his books one day, perhaps the consequences will be enough that he won't be likely to forget them again.

The partnership between you, your child, and his teacher is never more important than it is in the first few years of school. Your six or seven year old is launching a lifetime of learning and you want to be there every step of the way. One of the most significant things you can do to help your child become a successful, independent learner is to encourage good homework habits in the first and second grades.

The goal of first-and second-grade homework is two pronged: to build essential study skills—such as following instructions, beginning and completing assignments, and managing time—and to reinforce what was taught during the day. The discipline of mastering these skills does not come easily to six and seven year olds, which is why it is so important that parents become involved in the process. Although it may be your child's responsibility to bring assignments home, do the work, and return it to his teacher, it is your responsibility to make sure that homework gets done. Luckily, there is plenty of sound advice in this chapter about how to establish a homework environment and routine that will consistently support your child's efforts.

A positive attitude and the willingness to be a little flexible about your schedule—whether you work in or outside of your home—will go a long way toward giving you much-needed time to spend with your child as her homework partner. Enjoy the opportunity to share each other's company.

5

Sample Classroom Lessons and Homework Assignments

▼

I t's probably been quite a while since you've spent any significant time in an elementary school classroom—not since your own school days, if you're like most parents. And when you think back, you may not even be able to remember much at all about your educational experiences in first and second grade. That makes it tough to imagine what your child's every day struggles with schoolwork must be like. If only you could put yourself in your child's shoes for a little while, maybe it would be easier to understand what some of those challenges are and what you can do to help him rise to them.

This chapter offers you a way to do just that: The lesson plans reflect actual classroom learning experiences designed for young students and are written in a format used by many teachers to organize, structure, and plan activities for their classes. Sidebars in this chapter contain even more insights for parents from seasoned first- and second-grade teachers.

Of course, not every classroom lesson will follow plans as structured as the ones here, but every teacher creates some kind of lesson plan to work from as the day progresses. The sample plans in this chapter will give you a glimpse of the kinds of reading related activities that may be going on during your child's school day. If you have questions about them, or if you feel that your child isn't "getting" what is being taught in the classroom, don't hesitate to speak with your child's teacher. She may be able to give you good hands-on suggestions for remedial reading work at home. In any case, the bond between you and your child will be strengthened if you make the effort to understand what he is doing every day at school. If your child knows that you are aware of what is expected of him and are eager to help, his confidence and motivation to learn are bound to deepen and expand as he matures both as a student and a person. You may also note that your child's homework assignments vary a great deal, from textbook-based, fill-in-the-blanks worksheets to free-form book reports. Pay close attention to the kinds of assignments your child's teacher is sending home. Discuss them with your child and be sure that *both* of you understand how the homework exercises reinforce concepts that were taught during the school day. The sample assignments that follow should give you a better sense of what some of those concepts are. Read them carefully and look for ways to reinforce what your child is learning at school. Speak with her teacher if you have concerns or if you would like advice about things you can do to help support classroom efforts. Chapter 6 is full of ideas for games and activities that your child will enjoy at home or on the road. All of them are designed to encourage your first or second grader's comprehension and enjoyment of words, language, and literature.

FIRST GRADE

Sample Classroom Lesson Plan #1

Phonetic Spelling
Time: 1 hour
Materials: Consonant Sound Card, Family Words Worksheet

The objectives of this lesson are to:
1. Create and read words using a Consonant Sound Card
2. List all the words in twelve related word families
3. Practice decoding skills on real and constructed single-syllable words
4. Learn about exceptions to the rules of spelling and pronunciation
5. Learn new vocabulary

Setting the Stage

To begin the lesson, the teacher introduces the Consonant Sound Card, a 3-by-5-inch index card to the class. The fifty-three initial consonants and consonant blends that occur in English are written around three edges of the card.

Consonant Sound Card

start here

① ② ③

name

b c d f g h j k l m n p qu r s t v w x y z

Next, the teacher tells the class how the card is used: The Consonant Sound Card shows all the initial consonant sounds a word can have. If you match any consonant sound on the card to any vowel sound/final consonant sound combination, you will get a pronounceable word—not necessarily a meaningful word, but a pronounceable one.

Now the teacher passes out the Family Words Worksheet. This is a chart that lists all the vowel sound/final consonant sound combinations in a particular word family—for this lesson, it is the short *e* family.

Short *E* Family Words Worksheet

▼

ed	en	et	eb	esk	ent	ence	elt	ell	eg	est	end

After the teacher describes how the worksheet is used, students match each initial sound of the Consonant Sound Card to the middle and ending sounds on the Family Words Worksheet. The students then decode the combined sounds and pronounce the word they've made. If it's a real, correctly spelled word, it belongs in that word family. Next, each student writes the word in the worksheet column beneath its ending sound. If the combination creates a nonsense word, the student moves on to the next initial consonant sound.

In order to show children how to decode words, the teacher guides them through a series of mechanical steps that shows them how to:

> ➤ Align the edge of the card with the first worksheet column to create words. The first word they will produce in this manner is "bed."
> ➤ Decode this first word by saying "buh-ed, bed."

The teacher then asks the class if "bed" is a real word and discusses their answers as a group. (Some children may see the word as "beb;" in this case the teacher discusses reversals and the difference between the final -b and the final -d sound.) Next, she brings the class to the conclusion that "bed" is a real word and instructs them to write it in the column.

Now the teacher shows students how to slide their Consonant Sound Cards up one line to produce the word "ced." This word is decoded aloud as a group: "suh-ed, ced." The teacher points out that the class has used the soft c rule successfully and guides them through the process of deciding whether or not this word is real.

In a logical progression, the teacher moves on to "d" and asks the class to decode "duh-ed, ded." Using the opportunity to reinforce rules of spelling and pronunciation that her students already know, she points out any exceptions to the rules, such as "ded" which does not belong in the "-ed" word family because it is correctly spelled "dead." The teacher instructs them to move on.

The same steps (as described above) are used for every consonant sound on the card: As each new word is decoded, the class decides whether it is "real" or "nonsense"—with the teacher's help, of course. Only "real" words are written in the boxes of the first column. When the class has gone through all of the fifty-three initial sounds on the card, the first column of *-ed* words should contain several words, including bed, fed, red, and wed.

If there is still time in the Phonetics Spelling Hour, the teacher

66In the process
of learning how to
spell phonetically,
children discover
something important
about our lan-
guage—that there
are rule-breakers.
For example, "-ind"
is "supposed to be"
pronounced with a
short i. And it is, for
the word "wind"—
but not for any
other word, not for
"find" or "bind" or
"blind." So not only
are the students
learning the basic,
standard vowel
sounds, they're also
learning that
English has many,
many exceptions to
the rules.**99**

—SUSAN TODD,
FIRST-GRADE
TEACHER

will move on to subsequent columns—"en," "et," "eb," and so on. As she did before, the teacher helps the children decode and discuss every word.

Construction

The objective is to create twelve lists of word families in a systematic way. The teacher gauges the speed at which the students are able to move through the process of matching consonants and consonant blends with vowel and final consonant sound combinations. It will probably take more than one class to complete the entire worksheet. But it is important for the class to take its time and work together, so as to reinforce one another's decoding skills and vocabulary knowledge.

To reinforce the students' knowledge of these newly learned words, the teacher may give them this homework assignment: Write each word in a family three times. For example, write each the "ed" words formed in class three times. Perhaps she will have them create a sentence for each word in the second column.

Display

As the students proceed through each of the vowel sounds' families, they are asked to keep their worksheets. Eventually each child will create a book cover for his own collection of word families. The worksheets and covers are stapled together into a book that each child can keep for future reference.

Sample Classroom Lesson Plan #2

Presidents' Day Venn Diagram

Materials: George Washington and Abraham Lincoln data sheets; blackboard or overhead projector; Venn diagram work-sheets

The objectives of this lesson are to help students to:
1. Learn about the lives of two important U.S. presidents
2. Use a Venn diagram to analyze data
3. Work cooperatively to choose information for their diagrams

Setting the Stage

To begin this lesson, the teacher reviews the data sheets on George Washington and Abraham Lincoln that the students have been coloring and collecting over a two week period.

Discussion

The teacher then asks the class to share some of the facts they've learned about either Washington or Lincoln. With their input, the teacher creates two lists of facts for each man, using the blackboard or overhead projector.

Construction

Next, students are asked to re-group the information they've gathered into lists. Using their Venn diagram sheets, it is up to the students to decide which facts are unique to Washington or Lincoln, and which aspects of the men's lives are shared.

For example, student's Venn Diagrams might contain statements such as "General in the Revolutionary War" in Washington's "circle" and "Leader during the Civil War" in Lincoln's "circle." In the center portion of the diagram, the teacher would expect to find a statement that applies to both men, such as "President of the United States." The intersecting circles in the Venn Diagram, below, illustrate the intersection of two sets of information and underscore shared data.

> 66 The children in my class learned a lot about the Civil War doing this exercise; they were fascinated by it. And of course it led us to maps of the United States and other resources. We really had fun with the topic. 99
>
> —SUSAN TODD, FIRST-GRADE TEACHER

Display

One way to show off first-grade students' understanding of a difficult concept, is to display their Venn Diagrams on Presidents' Day—right next to some of the more traditional illustrations and writing one might expect to see on a holiday bulletin board.

Sample Classroom Lesson Plan #3

Guessing Game

This lesson works best for *tactile learners*.

Time: forty-five minutes

Materials: twenty-six small brown paper bags, 3-D uppercase letters

The objectives of this lesson are to:

1. Learn about prediction
2. Describe the shape of each letter
3. Put letters in alphabetical order

Setting the stage

To begin the lesson, the teacher points to each of the letters of the alphabet. She then asks the students if they would be able to recognize each letter, not by seeing it, but by touching it. The teacher then gives each child a bag, which contains a form of one of the letters of the alphabet.

Instructions

One at a time, a student will place their hand in the bag. They are not allowed to look in the bag, they must only use their hands to determine which letter is in the bag. As the student feels the letter, they are to try to describe it to the class. For example, if they have the letter "Q" in the bag, they might say, "This letter is round, except it has a tail. Most of the edges of this letter are smooth." The student should have the opportunity to guess the letter in his bag, but if he cannot guess, his fellow students who have heard his description are encouraged to guess.

Construction

When the student or students are fairly certain about which letter is in the bag, the teacher writes the letter on the bag. When the students have made guesses about each letter, they have to put the bags, which now have a letter written on them, in alphabetical order. The teacher opens each bag to see if the students were correct about their guesses. If some letters are mixed up, say "L" and "T," discuss how they can be confused, because their shapes are similar. It is likely that the students who described each of these letters, used very similar adjectives.

Sample Classroom Lesson #4

Rhyming "Simon Says"

This lesson works best for *auditory learners.*

Time: thirty minutes

Materials: a list of rhyming words

The objectives of this lesson are to:

1. Follow oral directions
2. Recognize rhyming words by sound, not by spelling

Setting the stage

Following a lesson about rhyming words, the teacher asks the students to stand shoulder to shoulder in a long line.

Instructions

The teacher tells students how to play "Simon Says." The teacher explains that she will say, just for example, "Simon Says: bird." Then she will say, "Simon Says: word." If the second word she says rhymes with the first, everyone in line should take a step forward. If the second word she says, doesn't rhyme with "bird," for example, she says, "Simon Says: cat," and the students should stand still. Children will have to listen carefully to the words being said. They will also have to be able to follow the initial instructions so that they know when to take a step or stand still.

Sample Classroom Lesson #5

Word Search

This lesson works best for *visual learners*.

Time: thirty minutes

Materials: a highlighter for each student, an old magazine or newspaper for each student

The objectives of this lesson are to:

1. Find and identify spelling list words
2. Understand the relevance of what they are learning in class to real life print

Setting the stage

Once the teacher has presented the spelling list for the week, he will discuss the importance of each word to daily life. He then hands out a magazine, or newspaper and a highlighter to each student.

Instructions

The teacher assigns a word from the spelling list. The students have five minutes to look through the newspapers and magazines to find that word. When the time is up, students can count how many times they found that word. It is not a contest to see who can find the word most often, but rather a way to show the students the relevance of the words they are learning in the classroom.

Construction

The students can use safety scissors to cut out sentences that have the word in them. These can be glued to a sheet, which can be posted on the bulletin board. Children will have a visual reminder of the words of the week.

Sample Classroom Lesson #6

ABC Freeze Tag

This lesson works best for *kinesthetic learners.*
Materials: none needed

The object of this lesson is to:

1. Encourage students to think of new words that begin with different letters

Instructions

This game is best played outside, or indoors in a clear area. The teacher picks two students to be "It." The teacher also picks a featured letter for each round of tag. These students designated as "It" run around and "tag" other students. If a student is tagged, they must freeze. The only way for him to become "unfrozen" is to say a word that begins with the featured letter of the round. For example, if the round is determined to be the "L" round, a student would have to say "love" or "light" to become unfrozen.

SECOND GRADE

Sample Lesson Plan #1

Wolf vs. Pigs: Point of View Venn Diagram

Time: one hour

Materials: Venn Diagram worksheets and two storybooks: *The Three Little Pigs* by Paul Goldone and *The True Story of the Three Little Pigs* by Jon Scieszka

The objectives of this lesson are to teach children:

1. The importance of point of view in fiction
2. How to use point of view to support different versions of the same events
3. How to use a Venn diagram to analyze the similarities and differences between two accounts
4. To practice essay writing based on data from a graphic organizer

Setting the Stage

First, the teacher settles the class comfortably. Next he reads two versions of the familiar *"Three Little Pigs"* story: a classic version, such as *The Three Little Pigs* by Paul Goldone, and *The True Story of the Three Little Pigs* by Jon Scieszka, which tells a very different version of events from the wolf's perspective.

Instruction

Next the teacher asks the class to complete a large Venn diagram (drawn on the board or on an overhead projector) labeled "Pigs' Point of View," "Wolf's Point of View," and in the center portion, "Alike." The teacher reminds the children to think back on each story for details to use in the diagram. For example, the students might suggest "three houses" for the overlapping, shared portion of the diagram, "afraid to be eaten" in the pigs' circle, and "just trying to borrow sugar" in the wolf's.

Discussion

After the class has finished filling in the diagram, the teacher asks the children to step back for a moment and consider what it is that makes the stories so different? She guides them to conclude that the difference lies in who is telling the story—the point of view. The teacher then explains that authors use point of view in many ways: to make us think, to make us laugh, to make us feel angry or sad. The teacher points to the diagram the students have just made to show them that in a story or any kind of writing, point of view can change everything. She also makes the point that there are at least two sides to every story.

Construction

Next, the teacher asks the students write a paragraph about either the wolf's or the pigs' perspective on *The Three Little Pigs* story. He reminds the children to use their Venn diagrams for help in structuring, planning, and writing their essays. Just for fun, he urges them to decorate their diagrams with wolf, pig, and house pictures.

Display

After the students have exhausted every color in their crayon boxes, the teacher attaches each student's essay to his or her diagram and hangs it up for show.

> 66 When I read a traditional version of *The Three Little Pigs* to my class, they could tell me the whole story, they knew it so well. After reading another version, we made a Venn diagram to compare the two stories. This activity helped the children to see an old favorite from a whole new point of view. 99
>
> —LAURIE CHAMBERS,
> SECOND-GRADE
> TEACHER

Sample Lesson Plan #2

Pumpkin Adjectives
Time: forty-five minutes
Materials: paper, markers, giant pumpkin

The objectives of this lesson are to teach students how to:

1. Write using descriptive words
2. Define adjectives

Setting the Stage

Students bring in a pumpkin to be displayed in the school's hallway. Since the children have been reading books such as *Pumpkin, Pumpkin* by Jeanne Titherington and *The Biggest Pumpkin Ever* by Steven Kroll, the teacher uses this opportunity to teach the children about descriptive languages and adjectives.

The teacher instructs the children to observe the pumpkin. The teacher also tells them to think of words they would use to describe it.

Instruction

After the children look at, touch, and smell the pumpkin, the teacher tells them to sit on the floor and asks them for words that describe their pumpkin. To help the children brainstorm a list of words, she asks them questions such as:

➤ What does it look like?
➤ What is its shape?
➤ How did it feel?
➤ How would you describe its size?
➤ What kind of texture does it have?
➤ What is its color?
➤ What does it smell like?
➤ Does is it smell like pumpkin pie?
➤ How do you think it might taste?
➤ What are your favorite things about it?
➤ What are your least favorite things about it?

As the children share their descriptive words the teacher writes them out on large chart paper.

Next, the teacher asks each child to write one of the describing words with a marker on an index card and tape it to the wall behind the pumpkin; this way they may share their words with the rest of the school.

Then the teacher tells the class that all these words are *adjectives*, or words used to describe, or "modify," a noun.

Construction

The next day the class reviews the list of adjectives. The teacher tells the class to use the collected adjectives to rewrite the poem

Pumpkin, Pumpkin by changing the original adjectives with new ones they have chosen.

Pumpkin, pumpkin,
<u>Round</u> and <u>fat</u>.
Turn into a jack-o-lantern,
Just like that!

Display

Once the children finish their poems, they share them with the class and hang them up in the hallway with the pumpkins.

Sample Lesson Plan #3

Springtime Word Web
Time: one hour
Materials: journals, schoolyard, word web worksheets

The objectives of this lesson are to teach children to:
1. Practice observation skills
2. Practice listening skills in a group setting
3. Use a word web to organize ideas
4. Write poems based on their observations

Setting the Stage

The teacher opens the lesson by reading a brief poem about spring. She leads the students in an analysis of the poem's ideas: which of them might the poet have drawn from first-hand observation?

Next, the teacher asks for ideas on how a poet views the world: Anything and everything in a poet's experience could be used in a poem.

Taking Action

The teacher then leads the class outside to the play area. She asks them to spread out in the schoolyard. The children have ten minutes to look for signs of spring and make a note of them in their journals. The teacher asks them to look for specific sights, sounds, smells, textures, temperatures, tastes, or anything else they can experience on this particular spring day.

The teacher urges the students to circulate, but there are a lot of distractions in the schoolyard—especially on a beautiful spring day. To keep the children on task the teacher asks pointed questions and guides them to new elements they can observe.

Discussion

After ten minutes, the teacher gathers the class in a central area. Before asking each child to volunteer one observation, she gives the children a chance to wind down from all the excitement of such an unexpected outdoor venture. The teacher asks the children to be as concrete and specific in their thoughts as they possibly can be, and gives them lots of positive reinforcement.

Construction

Back in the classroom, the students choose the words that describe their most interesting and colorful observations and organize them into a web pattern on their worksheets. Using the word web, they compose a short free verse or rhymed poem.

Display

The teacher helps students decorate their word webs so that they resemble daisy blossoms. The poems are arranged in the form of flowerpots. The children's "flower poems" can then be displayed on the School's "Spring Has Sprung!" bulletin board for all to admire.

Sample Lesson Plan #4

Amelia Bedelia

This lesson works best for *visual learners*.

Time: forty-five minutes

Materials: chalkboard, *Amelia Bedelia* by Peggy Parish, storyboard
with examples, worksheets with storyboard on them

The object of this lesson is to:

1. Introduce the importance of communication
2. Give oral directions

Setting the stage

The teacher asks how many of the children take the bus to
school everyday. She tells the children that she thinks "taking the
bus to school" means that they carry the bus to school in their
backpacks. The teacher then introduces the children to *Amelia
Bedelia*. She reads the story to the students, making sure that each
student can see the pictures. In each picture of Amelia doing the
job wrong, the teacher asks what it looks like Amelia is doing. The
teacher then asks what the other character, Mrs. Rogers, really
wanted her to do. When the story is finished, she makes a list on
the board of all the jobs that Mrs. Rogers asked Amelia to do.

The teacher introduces the children to the storyboard which has
four categories. They are Mrs. Rogers' directions, What Amelia
does, What Amelia should have done, and Mrs. Rogers' new
directions

Construction

The students will fill in the storyboard. For example, the first
category will read "Dust the Furniture." The second will show a
picture of Amelia putting dust on the dresser. The third will show
a picture of Amelia using a duster to remove dust from the dresser. The fourth category will be completed by the children, as they
refer to the story about the new directions Mrs. Rogers gives.

Sample Lesson Plan #5

Mystery Letters and Words

This lesson works best for *auditory learners.*

Time: thirty minutes

Materials: a list of letters or words, blank index cards, pens

The object of this lesson is to:

1. Teach the importance of following oral directions
2. Heighten awareness of letter shape and formation

Instructions

The teacher will hand out five index cards and a pen to each student. The teacher will describe how to write a certain letter, trying to be as specific as possible. For example, for the letter "T," the teacher might say something such as, "Draw a line beginning at the left side of the card, moving to the right of the card. The line you draw should not touch either side of the card. Starting in the middle of the line you have already drawn, draw a straight line down, stopping before the edge of the card." Children can guess which letter they think the teacher was describing. They can compare how their drawing looks to what the actual letter was.

Sample Lesson Plan #3

Sentence Scramble

This lesson work best for *tactile learners.*

Time: forty-five minutes

Materials: pens, paper, safety scissors, blank paper

The object of this lesson is to:

1. Learn about main idea, supporting sentences, and conclusions
2. Enforce the importance of sequencing

Setting the stage

The teacher finishes a lesson about writing a paragraph and the concepts of main idea, supporting statements, and conclusion.

Instructions

The teacher instructs students to write a paragraph on a topic of their choosing. The paragraph can be about any subject matter, but it must have a main idea, at least two supporting sentences, and a conclusion. Each sentence must be written on a different line of paper. The students then cut out each line of their paragraph. Students can pair off and exchange their cut up strips. Each student will be responsible for placing the sentences in the correct order so that the paragraph is recreated.

Construction

When the sentences have been placed in their proper order, tape them to a sheet of paper and display them on the bulletin board.

HOMEWORK ASSIGNMENTS AND PROJECTS

First Grade

Main Character Book Report

To kick off this assignment, the teacher asks each student to choose a book from the "special-books" shelf. These volumes are pre-selected by the teacher for interesting main characters.

While the children are reading the books on their own, the teacher asks them to remember what was said in class about "main characters." She asks the children leading questions such as: "Who is the main character in your book? What is she or he like? Would you want to be this character's friend?"

After the children have finished reading their books, the teacher asks them to describe the main character, using a form such as the following.

Main Character
Book Report

Your Name _____

Book Title _____

Author _____

Main Character _____

What did the main character do?

_____

_____

_____

_____

Next, students are asked to glue their forms to the back of a brown paper lunch bag. When the bag is turned over, it can be used to make a puppet of the main character. Crayons, markers, paint, scraps of material or paper, buttons, foam board, or yarn can be used to decorate the puppets any way the children like. In addition, the teacher might suggest that the children consciously select and use decorations to tell their classmates something more about their book's main character.

Taking the time to construct expressive puppets is important because the children eventually use them to deliver oral book reports—where it's up to the puppets to do all the "talking." Children are encouraged to practice their reports at home and coach their "puppets" to talk about who the main character is and what he or she did in the book. It can be very freeing for some children to express themselves through a medium, such as a puppet, especially if they find more direct forms of self-expression either difficult or embarrassing. Using a puppet also gives a child the license to be dramatic—to play a role that allows him to be someone else for a while. If the text of his book report—and the thoughts that shaped it—come to life through the imaginative use of a puppet, he will have done far more than to simply meet the requirements of an assignment.

Letter Patterns

Most first graders already know many different letter patterns. To practice them and understand them better, the classroom teacher encourages the children to "play" with letters and the patterns they follow.

For example, the teacher might ask the children to write as many new words as they can out of these letters:

AUTUMN LEAVES

A great way to get unstuck and create words quickly is to use magnetic letters on the refrigerator at home. Or write the words on a piece of paper, cut the letters apart, and move them around to make new words.

Here are some words to get children started:

TALE
SALE
NET
VASE

Some of the words your child might come up with are: Late, Ales, Ten, and Save. Can you make more than thirty words?

Word Rainbows

For this assignment children are asked to find red, orange, yellow, green, blue, and purple crayons. The object is to make word rainbows with the week's spelling words by writing each letter of each word in a different color. The letters of each word are to follow "rainbow order," starting with red.

Second Grade

Comprehension Worksheets

In this type of assignment, second graders, who are now expected to place a higher premium on comprehension, are asked to complete one worksheet each night after reading a chapter together in class. The questions on the worksheet are designed to help the children remember what they've read and to show the teacher that his students understand what is happening in the story. They may be asked to recall what a character was wearing, or how an event in the story took place. Children are encouraged to go back to the text—to re-read a portion of the book if they need help answering some of the questions.

Weekly Wordshop Words

At the beginning of every week students are given a list of four new "Wordshop Words." The selected words, which are posted in a special place in the classroom, appear in the children's readers and are used in discussions of other subjects, too. During the week, they learn to spell and use the new list of words and every Friday they are tested on how to spell them.

Typically, a teacher asks her students to complete the following assignments each night of the week in order to master their Wordshop Words.

Monday: Write the words three times each.
Tuesday: List the words in ABC order.
Wednesday: Write one sentence for each wordshop word.
Thursday: Study the Wordshop Words and practice for
    Friday's spelling test.

Patchwork Quilt Book Report

Here, second graders are asked to choose and read any non-fiction book. Using a graphic organizer, such as a word web, the children are then asked to single out at least four important facts they learned from their book.

Next, the teacher asks each student to create a quilt square for his book, using the template below. The finished square should be twelve inches by twelve inches. Almost any material can be used for the squares, although paper might be the most convenient option. In any case, each square is turned so that it forms a dia-

> 66 Starting in January, I ask my students to use their Wordshop Words to write a four-sentence paragraph. In fact, one of the most important concepts we work on throughout the year is how to use a main idea and supporting details to construct a paragraph. 99
>
> —DONNA COOK,
> SECOND-GRADE
> TEACHER

mond shape. Each child writes the title and author of his book in the center box and writes one of the facts he's learned in each of the corners.

Next, the quilt squares are decorated with various symmetrical patterns—lines, rings, or shapes. The children can use markers, crayons, paint, or any other materials to create interesting original patterns. Other options include basing designs on quilts that were researched in class, or on ones that children use at home.

After everyone has presented her square to the class, all the pieces are connected to create a quilt of information to hang on the wall.

All the lesson plans and homework assignments in the world will not help your child become a better reader unless you, as a parent, begin reading to your child (and model reading yourself) from the time he or she is a toddler. Now, there is not even so much as a shadow of a doubt that a child's familiarity with books, words, and the stories they tell, is the key to a lifetime of learning. If you look closely at any lesson plan or assignment designed to teach first- and second-grade children how to read and comprehend language—whether it involves Venn Diagrams, word webs, puppets, spelling worksheets, or crayons—the common denominator is a book.

Fortunately, teachers are becoming more creative and adept at drawing children into the splendors and uses of a reading life. The intention of this chapter is to familiarize parents with the methods and materials that are most commonly used to accomplish that goal. Hopefully you have a better sense now of what will be required of your child and how you can help her cope with reading challenges both inside and outside the classroom. In the next chapter, parents will be offered a wealth of ideas and suggestions about how to encourage and support their children's efforts to decode, understand, and enjoy the world of words.

6

Fun and Games: Experiential Learning

▼

Hands-on learning of all kinds seems to be the rage these days, not only in academic circles, but also in schools all over the country—and for good reason. Learning through experience—"Experiential Learning"—gives children an *active* role in their education and helps them understand the connection between "real life" experiences and what is taught in school—whether it is reading, math, science, history, art, or any "formal" subject for that matter. Children are now encouraged to participate in their education and to see for themselves how their own lives and the world around them both reflects and acts on what they learn in school. Within the context of learning to read, it is especially important for children to make a connection between the text and what they already know, feel, and imagine.

"Experiential learning" may sound imposing, but in fact it's something your child has been doing ever since she was born. Every toy you let her chew on, every trip to the duck pond, the supermarket, or a friend's home taught her something about the world. In fact, everything she does and everything she did—even as an infant—qualifies as an experience that will contribute ultimately to her reading education. In short, experiential learning is a key factor in the development of a strong reader. Although it may seem like it at times, learning to read isn't just a matter of class work and book smarts. Theoretically, you *could* teach a child the mechanics of reading—letters, phonics, and words—in a locked room with drawn shades. But without any experience or understanding of the outside world, a child really would not be able to comprehend the ideas those words express. In order to make sense of any written story, a reader needs to draw on all of his experiences.

That's why it makes sense to give your child the most varied experiences you possibly can, so that her well of knowledge will be deep enough to make inferences and connections whenever she reads. And as she reads more and more that well will deepen.

To a young reader, a simple at-home experience can be just as educational as the most exotic foreign vacation. So along with the competitive, creative, and word-based games in this chapter, you'll find tips and hints on how to do "experiential learning" with your child—from making grocery lists and visiting museums to playing in the sand, inventing puns, drawing, and guessing "what's in grandmother's attic."

Whatever you do, don't call any of it "work!"

FUN AND GAMES AT HOME . . . OR ON THE ROAD

Almost any activity can be construed as a learning experience, as long as it engages both you and your child in conversation, thought, and action. The most ordinary task—cooking a meal, folding the laundry, or driving around town doing errands—can open your child's mind to new vocabulary words, analytical opportunities, cause-and-effect, and chances to predict outcomes. When you're making supper, engage him in reading the recipe. Ask him to analyze each step you take in folding a shirt or, perhaps, plan the route you should take to get to the mall.

Flashcards—a perennial favorite among parents, teachers and—yes, even children, can easily be converted into fun-to-play games such as Flash Card Story Time, Flash Card Concentration, and Flash Card Charades. They can also be used to help a child work through a particular skill that's giving him trouble. For example, if he's having a hard time remembering alphabetical order, give him a deck of flash cards and ask him to practice arranging them correctly. If he can't match upper-case letters to their lower-case counterparts, spread upper- and lower-case flash cards face-up on a table and play a simple matching game.

Word and story games are another fun and educational way to spend time together, especially when you're stuck in traffic or have an hour to spare in the doctor's office, a bus terminal, the airport—or anywhere!

The main thing is to enjoy a variety of hands-on experiences and games whether you're at home or on the road. Either way, you'll find plenty of play-to-learn ideas in this chapter.

ACTIVE GAMES

Flash Card Charades

SKILLS: *letter recognition, phonics, vocabulary*

Any type of alphabet flash card set, illustrated or not, will work for this game, which is great for group play. Each player takes turns being the "actor," while the other players serve as "guessers." The actor chooses a flash card, and then decides on an object, an animal, or an action that begins with the chosen flash card's letter. The actor displays the card to the guessers, who name the letter and make its sound out loud. Then the charades begin! Wordlessly, the actor pantomimes the chosen word. He may snarl like a lion for letter L, curl up into a ball for letter B, or do a Rockette-style kick for letter K. (You may want to allow sound effects if your players need extra hints.) The guessers shout out possible answers throughout the performance, and the first to name the mystery word is the winner. The winner repeats the letter and letter sound, and then gets a turn as the actor in the next round.

Dough Letters

SKILLS: *letter recognition, letter formation, spelling*

Children who learn best through touch and movement can be especially challenged as they learn reading skills. They need many opportunities to feel and create letters. But any child will benefit from learning with all his senses, not just with his eyes and ears, so this is a great game for every kind of learner.

You'll need clay, play dough, or even bread or cookie dough. Show your child how to roll the material into long, thin cylinders or "snakes." Then challenge him to make letters of the alphabet from the dough.

As each letter is completed, say its name and the sound it makes to reinforce those concepts. Put different letters together and say the blended sounds that they make. Join letters into simple words.

With some kinds of play dough you can bake the completed letters (to harden them), paint or decorate them, and use them later to help your tactile learner literally put her letters together as she hones her reading skills. Of course, edible dough can be baked too—but don't expect the cookie letters to last too long as learning tools!

Letters in the Sand

SKILLS: *letter recognition, letter formation, spelling*

Here's another way to encourage tactile and kinesthetic learners to practice their letters. You'll need some fine sand—from the beach or sandbox is perfect—or baby powder, flour, or cornstarch.

Pour the sand or powder on a smooth, flat surface, like a cutting board or desk. Use your fingertips to write a letter in the material. Ask your child to name the letter and say its sound. Then use the flat of your hand to sweep the powder or sand back into position, erasing the letter.

Soon your child will want to create letters himself. Encourage him to say them aloud, both their names and the sounds they make, as he writes them. Ask him to write out vowels, the entire alphabet, or simple words. Even a spelling review can be more fun if it's written in sand!

You can easily adapt this game to an outdoor setting. Just smooth a spot in a sandbox or on the beach and write directly in the sand, using your finger or a stick.

Spelling Cheer

SKILLS: *digraphs (a digraph is a pair of letters that make a single speech sound, such as ea in meat or th in path), spelling, sequencing*

You'll need a pair of toy cheerleader pompoms to lend an extra touch of realism to this game—or you can make a pair from shredded Kleenex or newspaper.

When your child (or you) needs to let off some steam, take pompoms in hand and get up on your feet. Lead your child in a call-and-response "Gimme an A!" cheer, for either letter-combination sounds or full words.

EXAMPLE:
Parent: "Gimme an S! Gimme an H! What does it spell?"
Child: "Shh!"

Parent: "Gimme a C! Gimme an A! Gimme a T! What does
   it spell?"
Child: "Cat!"

Jump around, shout, toss off a cartwheel if you remember how;
do anything you can to encourage your child to get up and cheer
along with you. Some kids especially enjoy forming the letters
with their bodies in the time-honored "YMCA" mode.

Soon your child may want to call the cheer herself, with you
responding. Enthusiasm really counts at this point—even if she
gets the spelling wrong, cheer vigorously before offering a gentle
correction.

A My Name Is . . .

SKILLS: *alphabetical order, memory, concentration*

This classic schoolyard game requires a ball and a quick mind.
It can be played solo or in a group. While bouncing the ball, the
player recites:

"A my name is _____
And my brother's/sister's name is _____
We live in _____
And we sell _____ "

It's the player's job to fill in each blank with an appropriate A-
word—a girl's name beginning with A, a boy's name beginning
with A, a place name beginning with A, and an object beginning
with A. For example:

"A my name is Alice
And my brother's name is Al
We live in Alaska
And we sell apples"

Once the first verse is completed, the player moves on to "B my
name is Brittany," "C my name is Cassie," and so on through the
alphabet. It can be pretty challenging to keep the ball bouncing as
you rack your brain for a place name beginning with D (let alone
X)! For group play, the ball can be bounced over to another person after each verse is done.

COMPETITIVE GAMES

Flash Card Concentration

SKILLS: *phonics, memory, patterning*

To play this game, you need two sets of alphabet flash cards that are blank or identically patterned on one side, like an ordinary deck of playing cards. A set of upper case/lower case cards will work well (or you can easily make your own sets with a package of index cards and a marker).

Make sure you have two cards for each letter of the alphabet—either upper case/lower case pairs or two identical cards. Then shuffle the cards and arrange them, face down, in a grid pattern four cards deep and thirteen cards wide. The first player chooses and overturns two cards at a time, searching for a matching pair. With every card revealed, the player says the letter's name, the sound it makes, and a word beginning with that letter: "W, wuh, water; T, tuh, truck." If no match is found, the cards are turned face down again and the next player takes a turn. If the two cards do match, the finder removes them from the grid and chooses two more cards. When the grid is finally cleared, the winner is the player who has collected the most pairs.

All kids love Concentration. Remembering which card is where is truly a challenge—even for an adult player—but it's one that most children can meet. The triumph of fingering *the* matching card, among many possibilities, is sweet, and the occasional lucky strike of an overturned pair on the first try lends the game a bit of the gambler's thrill. Also, the phonics drill that goes along with this game goes down effortlessly, as kids compete to fix the evolving pattern of the grid in their minds.

Alpha-Bits Spell-Off

SKILLS: *letter recognition, phonics, blends, spelling*

Letter-shaped cereal is a wonderful thing. It's sweet, it's portable, it's nutritious (sort of), and you can play dozens of learning games with it.

To play Alpha-Bits Spell-Off, give each player a bowl or small pile of the cereal—hold the milk. Set a two-minute-timer and ask each player to form as many words as possible with the letters. You might want to distribute plates or pieces of dark paper to be used as word-forming surfaces. When the time is up, ask each player read her or his words aloud. The winner, the person with the most complete words, wins a handful of cereal to eat. Then it's on to the next round. Both the competition and the reward help keep interest high for most kids.

Look out for letter-shaped cookies, which are sometimes sold alongside animal crackers and which also work well for this game. Alphabet soup can be used, too, but not without a bit of a mess. And, of course, there's the classic game that both children and adults love to play, "Boggle!"

Chess

SKILLS: concentration, sequencing, consequences

It may not be an obvious choice, but studies have shown that kids who are taught to play chess show improved reading scores. Chess hones a multitude of mental skills, including logic, reasoning, judgment, prediction, planning, and concentration. All these skills apply to the act of reading, particularly to reading comprehension. A child who can sound words out easily but is grappling fiercely with the comprehension end of things could benefit greatly by learning chess. It could let him make an end run around the problem by approaching it from a new, stronger angle.

If you don't play yourself, there may be a chess player in your family or among your friends. Ask around. Many chess devotees feel an obligation to pass the game on to the next generation. They are often happy to teach the rules to a child and a to play a few beginner-level games with him. Do try to find someone with a deep reservoir of patience, though—chess is complex, and it takes some time to learn.

Many schools sponsor chess clubs to teach the game to children and help them practice. You might encourage your child to sign up if your school already has a club.

If your child's interest in chess takes off, consider choosing Lewis Carroll's *Through the Looking-Glass* as a book to read together. The story is structured as a giant chess game, with characters and moves that even a beginning player will appreciate.

CREATIVE ACTIVITIES

Make a Word Book

SKILLS: *vocabulary, spelling, word recognition*

You'll need a primary grade, lined writing tablet, one with line guides large enough for your child to print in; a pencil; crayons or markers; construction paper or card stock; and a stapler.

Beginning readers understand and use hundreds of words that they can't read on sight, or even spell phonetically. But the physical action of writing a word, for many children, can help them fix it in their minds, establishing it as part of their sight vocabulary. And the more often they see it, the better they'll know it.

Making a wordbook gives a child this chance. The book is simply a list or log of words that your child has learned in a particular subject, or words that are somehow related. Begin by suggesting a topic that interests your child—a sport, an activity, a kind of food, whatever. Coach him to think of eight or ten words he knows that relate to the subject. Ask him to write the words in list form on the lined paper (you can help with spelling—it's important that the words are spelled correctly—but don't write them down yourself; writing is an important part of the process). Your child can draw a small picture to go with each word. Staple the pages together between sheets of construction paper (in order to make front and back covers), and voilá—a word book of his very own.

Anything and everything can be fodder for a word book. If you go to the ballgame together, your child will hear a wide range of new vocabulary—everything from "hot-dog stand" and "foul ball" to "stadium," "parking lot," "ticket taker," "batter," and "bunt." Keep a log of those words. The next day, start recording them. A memento of your trip to the ballpark becomes something much greater: a tremendous expansion of the sight vocabulary your child will draw on as he builds his reading skills.

As your child creates word books, he'll begin to grow more and more appreciative of words themselves. Some children love silly words such as "giggle." Some children are fascinated and mystified with words like "cafeteria"—there are so many letters! These are fun books to make. An ambitious child might even want to create his own mini-dictionary, making books of words starting with A, B, C, and so on through the alphabet.

A child can have several word books going at the same time. In this way, he can work systematically on food words, sports words, fun words, color words, animal words, directional words, and hobby words simultaneously. This allows learning to reflect a child's life experience and interests. Developing this skill lays a foundation for good creative writing.

Once your child has made a word book, encourage him to look through it often. Ask him to read it to you. Pull out his baseball book "for reference" when you're watching the game on TV. Check out his food book as you decide what to make for lunch. Show him how amazingly useful his words—*all* words—are.

Wacky Weekly Words

SKILLS: *vocabulary, spelling, creative thinking*

The weekly spelling test remains a staple of the primary-grade routine. Many teachers will assign a list of words that the students will encounter in a story that week, or that form a "word family." Since repetition and review is a key component of spelling skill, the weekly words often crop up in classroom and homework assignments all through the week (see Chapter 4).

Wacky Weekly Words supports the learning process in a fun way. With the list in hand, challenge your child to create a sentence using as many of the weekly words as possible. This can be tough, depending on the length of the list and the words themselves. But this game values creativity, so bizarre sentences are perfectly acceptable. Take turns as the sentence-creator and "keep score" for one another as the words are used.

EXAMPLE: The weekly words are:
Bee
Tree
Trip
Tube
Cold
Cow
Soda
Sing
Hug
Up

When you come up with a sentence that uses all the words—or if one sentence emerges as a clear favorite—ask your child to commemorate the occasion by writing it out and drawing a picture to illustrate it.

Peanut Butter and Jelly Sandwich

SKILLS: sequencing, prediction, writing, cause and effect

This is a game that's sure to get big laughs—at first. Then it will get your child thinking.

Give your child a piece of paper and a pencil. Ask her to write down, step by step, how to make a peanut butter and jelly sandwich.

When she's finished, settle down in your kitchen and have your child read the instructions to you. As she does, follow her directions to the letter, taking every word literally.

EXAMPLE
Child reads: "Put the peanut butter on the bread."
You: Pick up the jar of peanut butter and place it on top of the loaf of bread.

Your child is bound to laugh at this ridiculous sight and say, "You know what I mean." Keep going through the original directions and see what kind of silly concoction you end up with.

Now, your child should see how important it is to think things through and use words exactly. Have her rewrite her recipe to be more specific.

EXAMPLE:
Child reads: "Place the knife in the peanut butter jar and remove it with peanut butter on it.
Using the knife, spread the peanut butter on the slice of bread."

Now make a real peanut butter and jelly sandwich using the revised directions and enjoy a snack together.

You can adapt Peanut Butter and Jelly Sandwiches to many situations. Challenge your child to write out directions for making other kinds of foods, playing various sports, or performing everyday tasks. If she really enjoys the game, she'll love the *Amelia*

Bedelia book series about a maid who takes all her instructions literally—with similarly hilarious results.

Alternative:

Write each step of the directions on a separate strip of paper (including some "silly" steps, if you like). Give the strips to your child and ask him to put them in the "right" order. Next, ask him to read each step out loud, as you assemble the peanut butter and jelly sandwich. If the sandwich doesn't come out the way it should, have a laugh—then ask your child to write (or dictate) the correct sequence for each step of the directions.

TRAVELING AND WAITING-ROOM GAMES

Roadside Alphabet

SKILLS: observation, alphabetical order

This game is perfectly suited for play in the car on long road trips—especially once you leave the interstate and start passing through towns and business districts. The object is to work through the whole alphabet—letter by letter—by spotting a word or object beginning with A, then B, then C, and so on. (Words printed on signs, trucks, or store windows are especially helpful for some players, so be sure to point them out.)

The group only needs to find one object per letter, but you have to actually pass that object while you're looking for its initial letter; the billboard you noticed forty-seven miles ago cannot be cited now for the letter B. So allow for plenty of searching time. (This game is a great choice if you're traveling with more than one child—two or three children are less likely to bother each other if they're staring intently out of windows.) And to minimize frustration, don't start playing until you're on a road where there's a lot to look at. But as soon as you can spot an apple tree, a bridge, a cow, and a dump truck . . . you're on your way!

Flash Card Storytime

SKILLS: phonics, sequencing, logic, story structure

Using a deck of illustrated alphabet or whole-word flash cards, choose three to five cards at random. Ask your child to tell a story featuring all of the items pictured. The tale can be as elaborate as your child wants it to be, or as simple as a brief paragraph.

Example: You draw the cards P for pig, G for Gate, and B for bus. Start your story by reviewing the words' initial letter sounds and revealing your special words to your listeners: "Puh, pig; guh, gate; buh, bus." Then the fun begins. "Once upon a time, there was a bus driver who drove his **bus** past the same farm every morning. Every morning, waiting behind a **gate**, would stand a huge pink **pig**. The pig would look sadly at the bus as it passed her by. Once the bus driver even thought he saw a tear in her eye. Finally one day the bus driver could stand it no more. Feeling sorry for the poor pig, he stopped right in front of her gate. The pig was overjoyed! She burst through the gate, hopped onto the bus, and happily rode it to the next farm down the road, where she went to visit her sister. The End."

Take turns drawing cards and spinning tales with your child. Be sure your own stories include such helpful sequencing cues as "Once upon a time," "The next day," and, of course, "The End." Fantastic twists, personal references, and the appearance of favorite characters or places can all add to the fun.

For a larger group—for example, in the car on a family trip—try "Flash Card Storytime: Pile-On." Pass the deck of flash cards around as each player chooses one card and adds a sentence or two to an ever-building group story.

Alpha-Bits Guess-the-Letter

SKILLS: spelling, phonics, reasoning

Take a small bag of letter-shaped cereal or cookies along on your travels, and you've got a learning game and snack rolled into one.

Guess-the-Letter is especially good when children are both bored and peckish. Begin play by pulling a letter out from the bag. Hide it from everyone else's view. Then give a simple clue or two that will help the other players guess what the letter is.

EXAMPLE:
Question: "This letter is all straight lines. It is the second letter in the word 'stop.' What is it?"
Answer: "T"
Question: "This letter makes the 'uh' sound in the word 'plum.' What is it?"

Answer: "U"

Question: "This letter makes the 'sh' sound in the word 'ocean.' What is it?"

Answer: "C"

Depending on the skill level of your players, you can vary the questions' difficulty widely, as above. You can also allow for questions and guesses ("Is the letter also in the word 'towel'?").

Whoever guesses the mystery letter correctly gets to eat it. That person also becomes "it," chooses the next letter, and asks the next question.

The Rhyming Game

SKILLS: *word families, listening*

This enduring classic is fun for all ages, and anyone who can speak can play. You need no materials—just voices and minds, so it's great to play while driving, waiting, or doing chores. Not only that, it also reinforces crucial reading and language skills.

The game is simplicity itself. Someone starts with a word, any word. You can take a cue from a roadside sign or a song on the radio. Players then take turns naming every word they can think of that rhymes with the starting word. Keep taking turns and naming a new rhyme each time around.

EXAMPLE: "Moon."
"Soon."
"Spoon."
"June."
"Noon."
"Tune."

For most children this age—and for non-competitive play—a round lasts until the group gets bored and a new word is suggested.

You can play a competitive variation, Tournament Rhyme, if it's better at holding your child's interest. The basic game is played the same way, but players must drop out when they can no longer think of new rhymes. The last rhymer standing is the winner.

Last-Letter Links

SKILLS: *letter sounds, spelling, concentration, listening*

This round-robin game is great for group play. No materials are needed, although it is helpful to have a scratch pad or erasable marker board on hand for younger players.

Begin by choosing any topic: boys' names, states and cities, or foods, for example. Player 1 begins by naming any word in the category. Player 2 must use the last letter of Player 1's word as the initial letter of another word in the category. Player 3 uses the last letter of Player 2's word, and so on.

EXAMPLE
Player 1: "hamburger"
Player 2: "rice"
Player 3: "eggs"
Player 4: "spaghetti"
Player 1: "ice cream"

Young spellers (and even older ones) can sometimes have a hard time figuring out the last letter of a word, so encourage them to write it out on a scratch pad when they get stuck. Answers cannot be repeated, so give players plenty of time to think. When everyone seems to have run out of words, just change the subject and keep on playing—the possible topics are limitless.

I Spy

SKILLS: *observation, listening, vocabulary*

The quintessential waiting-room game, I Spy sharpens children's observational skills, whether played one-on-one or in a group. At the same time, the activity encourages children to expand their vocabulary by associating new words with objects and their characteristics. One player begins by mentally choosing an object in the immediate environment, one that is within all the players' line of sight. She says: "I spy with my little eye something that's . . . " and names a quality of this object—its color, its initial letter, its size, and so on. The other players proceed to guess what the object might be, based on this clue.

EXAMPLE: "I spy with my little eye something . . . green."
"Is it the chair in the corner?"
"That magazine cover?"
"The plant on the desk?"

Whoever guesses correctly gets to choose the next object and be the "spy."

If you enjoy the game, be on the lookout for the *I Spy* series of books, which gets kids to search for objects within a complicated photograph, and the *Look-Alikes* books, which transform ordinary household objects into wonders.

Riddle Me This

SKILLS: *analysis, critical thinking, observation*

A kind of open-ended "Twenty Questions," this verbal game is great for travel time or whenever you're on the move. It works best if all the players can look at a map or picture (in a book) that is large and busy enough to contain many guessing possibilities.

You can start things off. Look at the chosen picture and choose one detail within it.

EXAMPLE:
Question: "I'm looking at a person in the picture who is
    standing up."
"Is it this woman with the dog?"
"The man in the straw hat?"
"The woman all in black?"

The player who guesses correctly wins and is given the chance to choose the next mystery detail.

By the way, the detail you choose doesn't have to be something purely visual. Depending on the picture, you can ask the players to find a person who looks sad, a color that seems peaceful, or an animal that might be hungry. Ask the guessers to give reasons for their guesses, if you go this route, encouraging them to consider and describe their thinking processes.

Grandmother's Attic

SKILLS: concentration, memory, listening, letter recognition, alphabetical order

This game works best with a group of three or more, but two can play just as well. Using the letters of the alphabet—in sequence—players take turns to create an imaginary inventory of objects they've found in Grandmother's attic. But before a player can add a new item to the alphabetical list, he has to repeat accurately all the items that have already been found.

Player 1 begins: "In Grandmother's attic I found . . . " any object beginning with the letter A: " . . . an aardvark."

Player 2 continues: "In Grandmother's attic I found an aardvark and . . . " any object beginning with the letter B: " . . . a baseball."

You can add to the fun—and the challenge—by including an alliterative adjective along with the object's name: "In Grandmother's attic I found an aardvark, a baseball, and some *chewy candy*." All subsequent players will have to repeat both of these "C" words, along with all the others, in order. So Player 4 might say: "In Grandmother's attic I found an aardvark, a baseball, some chewy candy, and a *difficult dinosaur*."

This game is great for practicing alphabetical order, of course, but very often it encourages some vocabulary one-upmanship, too, as players compete to "find" the most outrageous attic items.

Younger players can be coached a bit on the memory component of "Grandmother's Attic," and the game can continue for as long as their interest holds. With older children, who can handle an element of competition, you might want to eliminate any player who becomes stuck and can't repeat the list of items correctly.

READ-ALONG GAMES

Guess the Ending

SKILLS: prediction, analysis

This is a game to play before you begin to read a new book—or even crack the cover. Look at the book with your child. Examine the cover illustration together and point out what you notice about it. Look critically at the typeface. Notice the author's name: Have you read any of this person's work before? What was it like?

Read the publisher's description of the book on the back cover or the jacket flaps. Don't forget to look at the quotes from reviewers. (This can be a good opportunity to do a little consumer empowerment exercise. Think about who wrote that description and chose those quotes. How was that person hoping to make you, the reader, feel?) Talk about your expectations of the story.

Now, put it all together. What do you think this book will be about? And—a hard question—how do you think the story will end?

You can just talk about your ideas and predictions, using the conversation as a bit of a warm-up, before you begin to read the story, or you might want to make more of a project of it. Ask your child to draw a picture of what she thinks the book will be like; after you've read the story, she can draw again, this time expressing her reactions to "the real thing."

Here's another variation. On small slips of paper, you and your child can jot down guesses about the plot—either how the story will end, or events you think might happen along the way. Seal the slips in an envelope and set it aside. When you've finished the book, you can unseal the envelope with great ceremony and look back at the slips to see whose predictions came closest to the actual story.

Or you can work on a version of this form, which many teachers use with their reading groups to stimulate discussion and creative thinking as they prepare to begin a new book.

What do I see on the cover?

*Predictions*_____

_____

_____

_____

_____

*What did I noticed?*_____

_____

_____

*What would I like to find out?*_____

_____

_____

_____

Draw It!

SKILL: comprehension

Everyone communicates differently. Some of us are more comfortable expressing ideas verbally; others prefer writing. And some people—particularly some young people—aren't too comfortable using words at all. Children who are still working on the complicated rules of our language may resist using words out of shyness, uncertainty, or a reluctance to be wrong.

Art can reach these children in a way that nothing else can, and in fact most children this age can benefit from the expressive freedom that a box of crayons and a blank piece of paper offer. Draw It! is a great way to encourage your child to reflect on a story as you read it, and it's as simple as can be: After you've read a book or a chapter together, ask your child to draw a character from the story, a place that has been described, or the most interesting, exciting, happy, or scary thing that you've just read about.

If your child still shows interest, talk with her about her picture after she has finished it, and gently encourage her to describe more about the story as she explains what she has drawn. Label each page with the date and the book your child reacted to. You can collect all of her "story pictures" and make an ongoing reading scrapbook out of them; most kids love to look back over their own creations, and when they do they'll be reviewing the books as well.

Drama Club

SKILLS: comprehension

There's nothing like getting into character when you want your child to get into a book. A great way to do that is to give him the part of the hero (or the villain, as the case may be) and ask him to read that character's dialogue while you read him the rest of the story.

Don't hold back your own sense of theatricality: as you read, interject sound effects and as much emotion as you can muster. Your child will be that much more passionate about the story. When you feel his interest and know that he can look over your shoulder and follow along as you read, invite him to choose a character of his own. Then read on, pausing at his character's lines. Encourage him to read them with feeling.

Your child is more likely to be interested in the plot when he's directly involved in it. But be careful not to get *too* carried away with sound effects and voices—try not to lose your place in the story!

What'll Happen Next?

SKILLS: *inference, context, analysis, sequencing*

When an attack of the squirmies hits your child during a reading session, or if it looks as if her attention may have drifted elsewhere, a quick thinking exercise can work wonders. It will give your child enough of a break to let her snap out of her boredom (or daydreams) and get back on track, ready to read or hear some more.

The trick is the element of surprise. Wherever you are in the story, stop suddenly and announce a time-out. Then inquire, "So what do you think will happen next?" or "Guess what the character will say to that."

This technique is a great way to gauge your child's understanding of the story. It also helps him practice his critical reading skills, and demonstrates his ability to comprehend context clues and make predictions.

You can also play around with the questions by encouraging fanciful and imaginative responses. Ask, "What do you think is *not* going to happen next?" Or you can make a bizarre prediction of your own: "I think a blue cow will appear in their living room." After a little laughter you can jump right back into the story.

Another variation on "What'll Happen Next" is to break into the action of a story and ask your child what *she* would do next if she were Harry Potter. Take a minute to really get into the character's shoes. Then brainstorm together and imagine the character's response to any of these or similar questions:

How do you feel at this point in the story?
What could you do about your problem?
What do you need to know or learn to solve it?

You'll have a much more interesting conversation if you get involved in what the character *imagines*, as well. Alternatively, you can pretend to be a reporter and "interview" your child in character. Not only is this a wonderful challenge of your child's analytical skills, it's a subtle test of his comprehension as well.

Or, you might imagine yourselves as your book's villain or as a supporting character. These alternate imaginary points of view could give you both some fascinating new insights into the story.

EXPERIENTIAL LEARNING

The following examples of experiential learning are as much fun and just as valuable as the creative games and activities that are discussed above. However, the kind of "learning" they explore involves more "every-day" types of experiences, such as cooking, grocery shopping, visiting zoos, museums, aquariums—even gardening or going on a hike. There is a surprising amount to learn—and enjoy—from all of them.

Cooking

SKILLS: sequencing, comprehension, decoding, prediction

Perhaps the all-time best educational experience you can share with your child is cooking—precisely because it is such an ordinary, everyday task. All it requires, apart from the ingredients, is a little patience and time. Involve your child in preparing meals as often as you can. First, give him a chance to see the ingredients before you combine them. If you are following a recipe, ask him to read it to you as you assemble all the ingredients you'll need. Point out how important preparation and organization can be, and let him practice problem-solving ("What do you think we could we do if we mixed everything together and then found out we didn't have enough eggs?").

Ask your child to measure and compare the amount of each ingredient. Show him how ingredients are mixed in a certain order and let him knead or stir them to get a sense of what food feels and looks and smells like before it is cooked.

Talk about what happens to food when it cooks, and let him peek at it every now and then so he can see for himself. Challenge him to make up a new name for the recipe you just put together.

While you're talking about food, let your child read through your cookbooks and recipe collections. He may want to pick out another recipe—or even a whole meal—you can try together. If there's a special dish he really wants to make (and eat!) encourage him to write a list of the ingredients you'll need to make it. Ask him to look at the calendar to decide when to prepare it, and then write place cards for the table. All these tasks involve key literacy requirements: comprehension, writing, sequencing, prediction—the works.

Grocery Shopping

SKILLS: comprehension, comparison

Any task, done consciously, can be a learning experience for a child. Grocery shopping is especially productive for reading support, because of the nature of the typical supermarket: aisles are numbered and labeled, signs and words are everywhere, and a child who's concentrating on a task is much more likely to be involved in the procedure.

Constructing a grocery list is a wonderful planning exercise. Giving your child a day's notice, ask him to look at the pantry and refrigerator shelves and write down all the food items he thinks the family will need for the next week. When he has finished, go over the list with him to help him refine his planning: "I see you wrote 'apples,' but how many do you think we'll need?" "I usually use eggs in recipes. Should we add that to the list?" "Maybe you should choose one kind of cookie, not five . . ."

If you prefer, give your child a short list of five items or so to watch out for. Make his list very specific, including both the type of food and any brand names you prefer. Ask your child to figure out where each item is likely to be. In the produce section? In the freezer? Near the tomato sauce? Point out the overhead aisle signs. Then give him the responsibility of informing you as soon as he discovers one of the items on his list. (The idea is *not* to have your six or seven year old roam the store alone.)

When you've made it to the proper aisle, ask your child to find your brand on the shelf. Show him how to compare varieties, sizes, and prices. Then ask him choose the right item.

Finally, since good help is so hard to find, why don't you let your child choose a treat for himself? When you get home, ask him to help you put the groceries away so that he can see the end result of all his planning.

Hiking

SKILLS: comprehension

Nature is an invaluable resource for countless reasons—not the least for its importance as a learning laboratory for children. Comparing herself to a tiny ant, and then to a full-grown oak, can teach your child a lot about proportion and relative size. Observing a squirrel collecting nuts or a bird building a nest can help her think about sequences. Touching the leaf of a plant after a heavy rain or in the middle of a drought will help her understand cause and effect in a tangible way.

Bring along a small notebook and a pencil for each hiker, and encourage everyone to draw or jot down their observations as they walk. Some families make a point of keeping "nature journals" to boost their children's overall awareness and understanding of the natural world. If your child's interest in birds, bugs, or trees is piqued on this walk, she may want to continue using her notebook for backyard and neighborhood observations as well. Make it easy and fun for her to do just that.

If a particular animal or bird should cross your path, watch it and see where it goes. Talk about what it might be doing next. Your child might think it is searching for food or returning to its young. Encourage her speculation.

When you return home, plan an activity that will help your child cement her new observations. For example, she could paint a picture of something she saw on the trail. If you've taken photos on your walk, ask your child to help you label them once they're developed. If she has unanswered questions about the plants, animals, or places she's seen, organize a research trip to your local library—or consult the books you have at home—for more information.

Museums

SKILLS: comprehension

Going to museums is an excellent way to encourage reading because it both stimulates and satisfies a child's curiosity about the world beyond her immediate experience. Visiting museums (and libraries, too) will help give your child the idea that there is much to be learned and absorbed from a multiplicity of sources—some of them vast, beautiful, and infinitely fascinating—not just school textbooks.

There is one main rule of thumb to keep in mind when you are visiting museums with young children: go briefly and often. Trying to do too much in a single visit can be exhausting for small children and often discourages them from coming back. Instead, head for a particular hall or exhibit and spend time there, sketching a dinosaur bone, talking about the colors in a painting; or poring over hieroglyphs, for example. Help your child to concentrate on what she is looking at—you'll be amazed by how much she can retain when her interest is fully engaged. As much as you might want to stay longer, leave a museum while all of you are still having fun, and come back again in a week or a month to see more.

Art museums. Most children enjoy seeing works of art in beautiful or unusual settings. Before you go to an art museum, however, make sure that your child is aware of the ground rules: look, but don't touch; speak, but don't shout; and walk—don't run. Discuss the kind of art you are about to see. As you walk through the galleries, forego audio-tour tapes (which tend to focus on facts and details that don't interest young children) and instead carry on a running conversation with your child about the works you're seeing. Abstract art is a big hit with some children precisely because it isn't representational. A Pollock painting, for example, can be used as a jumping-off point for all kinds of conversations. Ask your child to observe a painting's colors and shapes, textures and size. Encourage him to describe its mood and feeling. Outdoor sculpture gardens are a wonderful alternative to most conventional "don't touch" museums because they allow children to experience art in a freer, looser setting.

Children's museums. Children's museums are decidedly not just for looking. Their hands-on exhibits are designed just for children, whether they explore science, art, nature, transportation, math, theater, or technology—to name just a few of the most popular themes. Try to avoid visiting museums during peak times—your child will be frustrated if it's too crowded to participate in hands-on exhibits. Also, be aware of varying age levels from exhibit to exhibit. You may want to steer him clear of those that are likely to bore or confuse him.

Historical museums. Few young children have much of a sense or appreciation of history, so it's best to visit a site or building that might reinforce what he's learning in social studies or American history. Some children especially enjoy historical re-enactments and "living history" museums. Keep an eye out for "kid-friendly" features, such as old-fashioned hats and period costumes children can try on or toys they can play with.

Natural history museums. For most children, the main attraction of any natural history museum is its dinosaurs, which hold an enduring fascination for most six to eight year olds. Look for as much interactivity as possible—some museums allow children to dig for "fossils" or project themselves into an animated ancient environment. Of course, the big bones themselves are quite a thrill. Dinosaur fossils have a way of showing up in the most unlikely places; so if your child is a fan, by all means search them out. Even if your child is not a dino-maniac, a museum's dioramas and other special presentations on the solar system, pollution, or evolution can reach a child in a uniquely tenacious way that will give him a background of understanding that he can rely on for years of reading comprehension.

Science museums are more hands-on than most traditional natural history museums and are immensely popular with some children. Interactive exhibits bring to life sciences such as physics and chemistry, which are often hard for young children to grasp. Some exhibits may be geared for slightly older children, however, so be sure to participate along with your child, if she has not been exposed to much science yet in the classroom.

Special interest museums. Look out for small, specialized exhibits in your home town or wherever you may travel. There are doll and toy museums, military and farm museums, and even TV and movie museums. There's literally something for everyone. Follow your child's interests and you're bound to find something to engage her.

After visiting any kind of museum, ask your child to write or draw something about the experience to help cement the trip in her mind—even if she insists on drawing or describing the lunch you had afterwards rather than anything "educational." Help her collect these pages in a binder, scrapbook, or photo album. She'll enjoy paging through her own memory book, and each page will help her recall the things she saw and experienced that day.

Planning and Researching Trips

SKILLS: comprehension, organization, prediction

Whenever you plan a vacation, trip, outing—or even a chore—try to involve your child in the work. There's no better way to demonstrate the real-life importance of sequence, prediction, and organization.

Before you leave town on a vacation or visit, help your child do some research on the city or region you'll be traveling to. Try an encyclopedia, the Internet, or your local library—reference librarians are amazing allies in any search for information. You might ask your child to choose an activity that you can do in the area you'll be visiting. You could ask him try to figure out what the place might look like (is it near mountains or the ocean? Will there be palm trees or pines?). Or you could ask him to help you decide what to pack by researching the region's climate.

Even if you're planning a simple zoo or museum trip, your child can scope the place out before you go. Try to find exhibit information or maps online or at the library, then ask your child to decide what he would most like to see when you get there. Not only is this a good research exercise, it's guaranteed to sustain his interest in the exhibit for at least a few additional minutes once you arrive.

Zoos and Aquariums

SKILLS: comprehension

In some ways, a zoo or aquarium visit is like a museum visit. Zoos gather one type of thing together in one place so that people can observe and better understand them. The difference, of course, is that in a zoo the exhibits are alive—and that is much more interesting to a child.

As with museums, don't try to pack too much into a trip to the zoo. Focus on one type of animal—birds, primates, or big cats, for example—and try to really *see* them. Spend enough time to observe them closely as they move, eat, and sleep. Ask your child to look at the environment the zoo has constructed for the animal. Does it seem comfortable in its zoo home?

Many children know a surprising amount about exotic animals from TV and movies, so give your child a chance to show off her knowledge. Ask her where the lion lives in the wild, or what gorillas eat. Help her read the informational placard that the zoo provides to confirm or refine her knowledge.

On the way home, talk about your favorite animal of the day, or a new thing you learned during your visit. Ask your child to write or draw a "scrapbook page" to help him remember this zoo trip.

GENERAL ENCOURAGEMENT

Family Book Group

SKILLS: comprehension, oral presentation

Set aside a weekend afternoon or an evening each month to discuss the books you are reading as a family or on your own. Many authors can be read and enjoyed by children and adults alike; try C. S. Lewis's Narnia books, J. K. Rowling's *Harry Potter* series, or just about any of Roald Dahl's children's novels, for starters.

You might assign one family member to begin the discussion, or you may decide on a main topic ahead of time: "What did you think of the ending?" "Who is your favorite character?" "How did this book make you feel?" Then listen—really listen—to one another's reactions to the story.

Don't quiz your young reader on the story's details or demand a blow-by-blow recap. The important thing is to encourage her to articulate her thoughts about the book, and to show her that you value her opinions.

At the same time, don't hesitate to share your adult perspective on the book. You may pick up on elements of the author's style and understand allusions and nuances that she is still too young to grasp. The skill of critical reading only comes with experience, and you can give your child the benefit of yours.

Keep the conversation relatively brief—a half-hour or so is probably all that a young attention span can manage—and end your book group with a special treat (ice-cream sundaes are big at my house, but a trip to the playground might be what's right for you). And while you're still together, mark your calendar for the next book-group session. Keep them regular, and soon your child will be reading critically, gearing up for the chance to make her readerly opinions heard.

Letter Writing

SKILLS: *writing, spelling, composition*

There is still nothing quite like the pleasure of receiving real mail from someone you care about. But of course it takes two to make a letter-writing relationship. Encourage your child to get into the habit of being the sender, and soon enough he'll be a recipient too!

Ask your child to jot down one or two things she did, saw, heard, or learned at school. It doesn't have to be anything exciting or unusual; a simple detail is all you need. Afterward, put her notes in an obvious place (i.e. the refrigerator or a bulletin board), where they'll be easy to find the next day. When the weekend rolls around, reserve a half-hour during a lull in the day for letter writing. Some children are especially motivated to write if they have their own stationery, or if they've made it themselves. Help your child get settled in his usual homework spot, and tone down any surrounding distractions. Bring out the week's daily notes, sharpen a pencil, and encourage your child to write a brief letter about the week gone by.

Your child might want to send his letter to a different friend or relative every week, widening his pool of correspondents.

Grandparents, in particular, love to receive mail from their grand-children and are usually quite good about responding. Or there might be one special person with whom he wants to stay in close touch. Your child might even want to write to a favorite celebrity. Regardless, be sure to stress the importance of neatness and good spelling. Be on hand to help him with any questions that might come up as he writes, and let him address and stamp the envelope himself before he puts it in the mailbox. Finally, don't forget to be as happy and excited as your child is when he receives a response in return!

Finding ways to help your child learn to read is so important that you simply can't afford *not* to have fun! First and second graders are great lovers of goofiness, and nothing is as funny to them as a parent's attempts to capture it. Never hesitate to use silliness in your efforts to encourage your little student to perk up, pay attention, and learn.

This chapter has provided lots of suggestions to spark your child's interest and excitement in reading, whether she likes games that are active, competitive, creative, challenging—or all of the above! Virtually all of these games require your participation, which makes them all the more personal and valuable to your child. He will love sharing these learning experiences with you. And, in all likelihood, your child will bring his newfound enthusiasm for reading to the classroom.

The beauty of sharing even the most mundane activity with your child—taking a walk through the woods, traveling to a near-by town or even going to the supermarket—is that there are so many opportunities to learn something new. And all of this information "uptake" happens outside of the classroom! This is the very gist of "experiential learning." If your child's preferred approach to learning is hands-on be sure to give her as many experiences as you can, whether it involves going to museums, cooking meals at home, taking trips, starting a book discussion group or writing to a pen pal. Your excitement for life and experience—and your willingness to share and enjoy all of it with your child—is perhaps the greatest gift you can give him.

7

When You Need Expert Help

▼

No matter how hard your child is working or what you are doing to help him, a reading delay may be more than you can handle on your own. But don't despair—a great many professionals are out there, ready and able to help you. A key component is time. If you're concerned about a lack of progress, don't wait to seek help. The sooner you intervene, the better it will be for your child.

Another important component is patience: Try not to panic or rush your child. Many teachers feel that first and second graders need several months of work on a new skill before they can use it competently and confidently. Significant progress in reading and writing skills is rarely made over night. Indeed, for many six and seven year olds, learning seems to happen very slowly . . . and then all at once. Your child may simply need a little extra time to see, hear, and practice new concepts before, suddenly, understanding switches on like a light bulb. If he continues to progress slowly, however, persist, be patient, but don't pressure him. A decision to get outside help for your child, if you suspect a serious reading problem, should be arrived at gradually. However, there are several telltale signs that can help you make the decision.

WARNING SIGNALS

While you are giving your child the space and time in which to progress at his own speed, keep an eye open for some of the following symptoms, which could point to a serious reading problem. It is very important to note, however, that these symptoms should not cause undue alarm unless they are *chronic* and interfere with your child's progress. Almost every child exhibits some, if not all, of the behaviors listed below at one point or another. In other words, you can expect your child to be inattentive, bored, frustrated, unmotivated, or even refuse to read on occasion. The key factor in diagnosing a potentially serious reading problem is recurrence and regularity of symptoms.

Signs and Symptoms of a Reading Problem

- inattention
- refusal to decode
- inability to blend
- fear of failure
- a defeatist attitude
- reads without feeling
- can't retell a story
- experiences reversals
- lacks confidence
- daydreams
- recognizes words in one context but not another
- continues to "sound out" words that should already be familiar
- is easily frustrated
- experiences physical discomfort or pain while reading
- gives off-target answers to comprehension questions
- is not motivated to read
- procrastinates to avoid reading
- displays unusual behavior or emotional state while reading
- has trouble following directions
- trouble with sequencing
- makes up excuses to avoid school or homework
- unable to tackle homework without a parent at his side

OTHER FACTORS

Recognizing a reading problem is never easy, even if you have a list of symptoms to refer to or a pile of books to delve into. However, some of the factors listed below may have an impact on your child's ability to progress as a reader. None of them are irreversible and can be thoroughly addressed over time.

➤ **Immaturity.** Some children are just not developmentally ready for reading at the very moment the school curriculum expects them to be. In general, immaturity tends to apply to young boys more than it does to girls of the same age. And, as you might expect, it is usually more prevalent among children who are chronologically the youngest in their class. However, now that even the youngest schoolchildren are expected to perform according to higher state and national standards, problems with delays in reading readiness are becoming more common than ever. If your child finds it difficult to sit still for the length of time it takes to read a brief story, or simply refuses to decode new words, immaturity may be the cause. For some children, time can be an effective and safe way to cure immaturity, so don't be surprised—or offended—if a teacher or administrator suggests the possibility of holding your child back for another year of first or second grade. But do consider this decision very carefully before you make it. Many studies associate long-term social and intellectual problems with children who have repeated a grade. Holding back is never a cure-all, and always a last resort.

Immaturity: Boys vs. Girls

As a parent, I clearly noticed the difference in the social development between my daughter and my sons. Boys and girls mature at different rates. For example, in second grade, my daughter matured a lot, much more so than my son, who is currently in second grade. Not only did she mature more quickly, but her progress also began to show during first grade—earlier than his.

—A DAD FROM SEATTLE

➤ **Extreme disinterest.** With everything from television and video games to team sports and play dates competing for your child's attention, it's not surprising that reading and schoolwork are frequently last in line. But there may be other reasons why your child puts off reading or doing his homework. Fear is one possibility; some children are afraid to fail at reading—and so refuse to try. Lack of success is another potential cause; your child may need to read less difficult materials to help her gain a feeling of mastery and achievement before she can move on to more advanced works. If you can't pinpoint the root of your child's lack of interest—and if you've tried limiting household distractions such as TV viewing and computer use—consider a consultation with the school psychologist or another professional who has had extensive experience working with children.

➤ **Lack of confidence.** A string of failures early on in a child's reading career, absence from school (because of illness, for example) or a physical problem with vision or hearing can result in a learning delay. It's tough to feel so far behind your peers, if you've missed class time. And playing catch-up isn't easy when the class is continuously advancing. To help her overcome self-doubts, your child needs empathy, gentle encouragement, and as much one-on-one adult attention as you can give her. Read together, play word games, and reassure her that she's wonderful no matter what. Children who don't feel confident about reading can be helped by a private tutor. In fact, lack of confidence is probably the single most common problem that tutors see, but it is one they can truly help solve.

In order to build your child's confidence in his own abilities, encourage him with fun activities such as developing a play. The whole family can join in by retelling their favorite aspects of holidays or family trips, which can then be recreated into plays. Everyone can have a part. The play can be a simple one-act, or as complex as a set-filled and costumed extravaganza. Or, try using puppets!

GREAT IDEA!

➤ **Lack of comprehension.** Listen closely when your child reads aloud. Does he read with any feeling? Does his tone rise for a question mark, or emphasize an exclamation point? Does he pause for commas and stop for periods? If a story has been read to him, can he answer questions about it? Can he describe the plot to someone who's not familiar with it? Decoding without comprehension is a very common problem among young readers, and if you are seeing no improvement—even as you work through games and exercises involving prediction, sequence, cause and effect, and other comprehension skills—then additional help may be called for. Consider a tutor or a school-based remedial reading group.

➤ **Reversals.** It's common for young children to be thrown off by letters that look similar. For example, some children confuse lower-case "b" and "d," mix up capital "N" and "Z," or mistake "J" for "L." They may also write letters, or even whole words, backwards. In some children—but not all—this is a warning sign of dyslexia, a brain-based reading disability. Letter reversals usually fade entirely by the end of second grade. If you don't see a gradual decrease of reversals in your child's writing, or if you notice that he makes physical reversals as well (i.e. mistaking right for left and up for down), he may be experiencing perceptual problems, in which case, a medical assessment should be made.

Dyslexia is a learning disability characterized by problems in expressive, oral, or written language. Dyslexia is not a disease. Dyslexia is not the result of low intelligence. The problem is not behavioral, psychological, motivational, or social. It is not a problem of vision. Dyslexia results from differences in the structure and function of the brain.

—THE INTERNATIONAL DYSLEXIA ASSOCIATION

Educator Peter Cookson, Ph.D., elaborates, by saying that those affected by dyslexia "systematically reverse numbers or letters, perceive letters or numbers upside down, or reverses word order—for example, reading "was" for "saw."

LOVES THE PICTURES, IGNORES THE WORDS

Some children with quick imaginations and creative minds have little use for the author's version of the story. They prefer to concentrate on the art and make up their own tale. While other children, after years of watching TV and videos, expect a visual image to make sense of sequences and stories. Either way, the lack of interest in words can be a problem. One way to help turn it around is to hide the pictures (or use pictureless books), which, in effect, forces a child's imagination to work on the basis of words alone. Now might be the time to start a family read-aloud project with more advanced novels and stories. Look for books that will grab your child's interest. You may need to spend some time browsing the shelves of your local library for good candidates, but every moment you spend in the stacks is worth it, if, as a result, your child gets hooked on words.

Bestsellers

Thanks to J. K. Rowling's wildly successful *Harry Potter* series, children's books are back in the news. While this series is likely too advanced for first and second graders, it does appeal to this age group, especially boys. Why not get into the habit of reading a chapter to all the kids each night before bedtime? Once they catch the "reading bug," they'll likely want to try to read a book on their own. Some fantastic early readers that appeal to first and second graders include the following:

- *Bedtime for Frances*, by Russell Hoban (HarperTrophy, 1995)
- *Eloise*, by Kay Thompson (Simon & Schuster, 1969)
- *The Giving Tree*, by Shel Silverstein (HarperCollins, 1986)
- *Joseph Had a Little Overcoat*, by Simms Tabak (Viking, 1999)
- *Junie B. Jones and the Sneaky Peeky Spying*, by Barbara Park (Econo-Clad, 1999)

➤ **History of physical problems or illnesses.** Your child might be healthy today, but earlier health problems may be affecting her development in subtle ways that have gone unnoticed until now. Premature birth, frequent ear infections, severe allergies, and numerous childhood illnesses can affect a child's sensory development. These conditions are associated with later reading, auditory, and speech difficulties. Think back over your child's early years, or ask your pediatrician to review her medical records with you. This history may give you clues to the roots of your child's current problem.

SCHOOL ANALYSIS TEAMS

If you've seen any warning signs of a reading problem in your child, don't hesitate to bring them to the attention of your child's classroom teacher. In all likelihood she has seen them too. If she has, or if new or serious problems have developed, she may suggest that the school's in-house analysis team discuss your child's situation. Analysis teams are ad-hoc groups of educators that meet as needed, to discuss, analyze, and brainstorm solutions for the problems of individual students. The group usually includes the child's classroom teacher, other teachers who have expertise in the problem area, the school nurse, the school psychologist, remedial and special-education teachers, and the principal. Ultimately, the nature of a child's learning problem determines the members of the team, who then move on to explore various strategies and ideas about how to help the teacher help the student.

Before a teacher initiates a school-based team evaluation of a child's reading progress, however, he will have already spoken with the child's parents and tried a variety of strategies. Teachers and other school personnel simply don't move ahead with a remedial program for a child until everyone is on board—especially the parents. The teacher may make recommendations, but once again it is up to the parents to decide what is best for their child.

Depending on the school, or your district's resources, the analysis team may recommend remedial help for your child, or perhaps, a round of tests for physical and cognitive problems. These may be carried out within the school district's range of authority, but you may also opt to pursue testing on your own.

It can take time and persistence to schedule assessments and evaluate results. School bureaucracies can be monolithic and slow to move. A problem that is noted in October, for example, might be monitored through December, discussed by an analysis team in March, formally tested in May, and diagnosed in June—too late for remediation in that school year. This is not always the case, however—some schools and school districts move faster. The thing to remember is that teachers, administrators, and parents are generally on the same side, so try not to be discouraged by scheduling setbacks. Keep focused on the goal, which is to get your child the help and support he needs.

INDEPENDENT TESTING

For a second opinion, or to save time, some parents choose to test their child's abilities independently. Your medical insurance may cover such things, so be sure to check your policy.

If you suspect that a physical problem may be contributing to your child's difficulty, her pediatrician or your family doctor should be the first person you consult. Most medical doctors can perform simple screening tests for visual, hearing, and other problems right in the office, and all should be able to give you good referrals to specialists for further evaluation. Physical problems such as partial hearing loss, visual impairment, blood disorders, and allergies are surprisingly common causes of learning delays—and are surprisingly easy for children, masters of the resourceful coping strategy, to mask. In fact, many educators advocate vision and hearing tests for all children by the time they enter first grade.

Education specialists or child psychologists are best equipped to diagnose learning disabilities, such as Attention Deficit Disorder (ADD) and Attention Deficit Hyperactivity Disorder (ADHD) that have been much in the news in recent years. According to national estimates, approximately 2 to 4 percent of children suffer from these disorders. It is important to note, that ADD and ADHD are not *learning* disorders, they are behavioral disorders that in turn affect a child's ability to learn. For example, a child with ADD may have difficulty paying attention to the teacher, being distracted by anything else that catches his eye. A child affected by ADHD may disrupt the class or simply not be able to sit still for any appreciable amount of time. The debate centers on whether or not children are being over-diagnosed and overmedicated for this disorder as a result. However, there are legitimate reasons to pay attention to the debate, especially where treatment is concerned, if your child is experiencing any of the symptoms that are associated with ADD. In any case, it should not be dismissed as the syndrome *du jour* or considered a mere treatment fad. For a valid diagnosis of your child's reading or learning disability you may want a second, or even a third, opinion from a seasoned child psychologist or education specialist.

DO-IT-YOURSELF ASSESSMENT

A number of books and Internet sites offer tests you can administer to your child at home for evaluative purposes. One site dedicated to selling assessment materials is www.assessments4kids.com. The subjects tested include both reading and language arts. Funbrain.com also offers practice quizzes for first through eighth graders. Finally, www.explorasource.com offers materials that are intended to "find resources to match specific learning needs and education standards. Many of these are designed to give home-schooling parents placement guidelines for their child's unique academic program. But even if you're not planning to home-school, these tests can help you identify and understand your child's problem. Chapter 9 includes some home-testing resources to give you a starting point.

SCHOOL-BASED REMEDIAL HELP

Once it has been determined that your child needs an organized program to help her cope with a reading delay, look into her school first and investigate whether or not it offers remedial help. Many schools do, but the quality of programs varies widely from one school to the next. Sometimes remedial help is limited to the use of the Resource Room, which is a separate and interactive workshop environment where children with learning disabilities are brought from their classrooms to work on their skills, usually in a one-on-one or small group setting. Other schools have instituted more formal remedial reading programs or special education classes. Some classroom teachers make audiotapes and remedial computer programs available to students who need them.

Although there is no "typical" remediation program, it is not uncommon for teachers to organize small reading groups that are devoted to students who are struggling with their reading skills. Made up of only four to seven children, these groups are intimate, and the teacher strives to keep them supportive—a safe place for children to test their reading abilities. These special sessions are usually conducted outside of the classroom, while the rest of the class has its own reading lesson. The teacher chooses a book that has a slower pace or is less difficult than the rest of the class is working on, and the children read it together, chapter by chapter. Vocabulary is discussed and all kinds of questions are addressed, just as they would be in a "regular" reading lesson. The group doesn't use a textbook, instead the students read engaging chapter books that have strong plots and characterizations, the better to catch and hold their interest. The mood is light (when your teacher starts a lesson by pirouetting down the hallway in a cheerful game of follow-the-leader, it's tough to be glum), but the students take the work seriously, and they're kept on task with frequent breaks for context questions, predictions, and sequencing reviews. Everyone in the group takes a turn reading aloud, so the risk—and, in the end, the success—is shared, as is the joy of reading a good story together. A growing number of communities are recruiting local volunteers to mentor and read with children in their neighborhood schools, or organize after-school or summer reading programs in connection with nearby public libraries.

Some schools invest great time, effort, and funding in international programs such as Reading Recovery. Reading Recovery, established in the United States in 1984, is intended to help first grade students who struggle to read and write achieve skills appropriate to the class average level. Marie M. Clay, an educator and psychologist from New Zealand, first brought the program to Ohio State University. The program is designed to improve literacy through daily one-on-one instruction by a teacher specifically trained in intervention literacy. Intervention literacy is, simply put, a proactive approach to teaching struggling readers to become independent readers. The purpose of such programs is to help children "catch up" before the reading gap widens and affects their learning in later years.

Others have access to state- or district-run programs of small-group remediation in language, reading, and math. The content and goals of such programs can differ greatly, and their availability may also vary from district to district and school to school. To get a clear picture of all the resources that are available to your child, speak to a school administrator or your school district's main office, or contact your state's department of education.

OUTSIDE SUPPORT

Learning Centers

Many learning centers and other commercial education companies offer academic screening tests that can be useful in diagnosing your child's reading level. Bear in mind, however, that these
tests are created primarily as sales tools for the learning center or
education company. Therefore, it is important to look at the
results of these tests in that context.

In the last decade or so, the new emphasis on standards and
testing has spurred the growth of the test-preparation business.
This expansion has created a subsidiary boom in generalized
"learning centers;" these for-profit businesses offer after-school
courses meant to help children who are struggling in school and
offer enrichment to children who are doing well. The best-known
learning center chains—including Huntington and Sylvan—have
franchises across the country. They generally teach students in
groups, although some offer one-on-one tutoring services to the
youngest pupils.

While many teachers have seen students gain from their extra
work at a learning center, some question their value—is it the program itself that helps or just the regular sessions of distraction-free
time? In addition, these programs can be as expensive, if not more
costly, than a private tutor.

If you want to know more about major learning center chains,
you'll find contact information for them in Chapter 9.

Online Tutoring

While Internet university programs are exploding in popularity,
Internet elementary-school tutorials are racing right alongside.
Some sites offer daily homework help to members, with certified
teachers at the other end of the modem to answer children's questions and guide their work progress. Sites with guided multimedia
learning experiences for sale allow a student to put together his
own complete or partial curriculum. And there are dozens of
home-schooling programs online, many of which can be cus-
tomized to support any level of skill, whether it is reading or
math.

However, most Internet and online tutorials are much too
sophisticated for six and seven year olds. Internet learning
requires a great deal of self-discipline to work well—something
most first and second graders have in very short supply. The costs

vary widely, and there's no guarantee that staffing and other promises are real. Also, media-heavy Web pages take an eternity to download, as far as a six or seven year old is concerned.

Some sites stand out, though, and may give you some useful insights into helping your child. For example, E-tutor (www.e-tutor.com) offers online lessons in language arts (which includes reading skills), math, science, and social studies to kindergartners through twelfth graders. The lessons—more than 400 of them—are written by teachers, but the follow-through is entirely student-directed (live links to instructors are not included). This sort of program might be exciting for a self-starting student, but most first and second graders need human guidance.

Don't overlook the Internet as a resource (Chapter 9 provides a guide to some especially useful sites), but as a primary teaching tool for a young child it leaves a lot to be desired.

Reinforcement Materials

There is a vast range of workbooks, reading games, educational CD-ROMs, and other materials available to parents and students today. A local or online teacher's store should carry a good selection of these learning tools.

For easy access to teaching materials, go online and check out these sites:

- www.theteacherstore.com
- www.hammett.com
- www.rightstart.com
- www.zanybrainy.com
- www.noodlekidoodle.com

Sometimes a child is reluctant to do extracurricular reinforcement work if it's supervised by his parent, but will be happy to "play learning games" with almost anyone else. In cases like these, a professional tutor is probably not required. Many people are willing to follow workbook directions or play a computer game with a child. See if your child is willing to work with a familiar teenager, caring neighbor, uncle, aunt, or grandparent.

One-on-one Tutoring

Many primary-grade teachers maintain that private tutoring remains the best solution for young students who are struggling with reading. Many children at this age just don't work well in a large group. Some feel lost as one voice among twenty or more peers, and they have a hard time taking the risks that go with any learning process. However, one-on-one tutoring time—even if it's only for an hour a week—can give them the confidence they need to work in a group environment each day at school. Other children find it almost impossible to concentrate amid the bustle and activity of the classroom. To progress they need distraction-free instruction time, something they just can't get at school. Children who have lost ground due to illness or an undiagnosed problem frequently need special help to catch up with their peers. In any of these cases and in many more, a private tutor can be the solution. (Chapter 8 guides you through the process of finding, choosing, and working with a tutor.)

Specialized Therapies

If there is any kind of medical component to your child's difficulties, you may want him to begin a specialized course of therapy or treatment tailored to his needs. The variations on these therapies are many, and may involve exercises, prescription drugs, and sensory aids such as glasses or hearing aids. Talk with your child's doctor about all the possible courses of therapy that are suggested for your child. Find out how long each one may take, its probable effectiveness, and any side effects before you choose one. And be aware that even when the physical problem is corrected or under control, your child has lost some valuable educational time. He may still be in need of tutoring to boost his confidence and help him catch up with his classmates.

Whether your child's problem is as straightforward as a head cold or as troubling as an allergy, you've learned to intervene as quickly as possible in order to head off future complications. A reading delay is no different: Early detection and treatment is paramount. But unless you know what the salient features of a reading problem are, you might not know how to determine if your child needs help, or what kind of help would be best suited to his needs if indeed he does have a reading problem. Hopefully, this chapter has helped to clarify the many assessment and treatment options that are open to parents today. In the end, it would seem that one-on-one tutoring is the soundest and most successful method of treating a first- or second-grader's reading problem. (Chapter 8 explores how to find a tutor, explains what they do, and suggests how you and your child can benefit from the relationship.) Perhaps the best advice this chapter offers is to keep an open mind to new suggestions and approaches. With so many techniques and professionals ready to help, your child should get exactly what he needs to start reading with more confidence and enthusiasm.

> **66**Kristin had vision therapy sessions once or twice a week for almost two years. She was having problems with convergence—seeing double—and that was one reason why she was having trouble with reading. Kristin also had a perceptual problem; she couldn't dissociate upper from lower, or right from left, so she would confuse b's for d's and so on. Her therapy involved sequence exercises, scanning practice, and exercises that re-trained her eyes to focus quickly and work together. After successfully completing her vision therapy, she continued to see a tutor once a week to continue building her confidence and reading skills.**99**
>
> —A MOM FROM NEW YORK

8

Hiring a Tutor

▼

Although there are any number of good learning aids and programs for children who are facing educational difficulties, most primary-grade teachers—as well as experienced parents—agree that the remedial needs of first and second graders are best handled the old-fashioned way: through the one-on-one, give-and-take dynamic of tutoring. Whether a child's reading problem is caused by a developmental delay, a lack of comprehension skills, or a poor grasp of phonics, instruction from a good tutor is frequently the best choice for a child in this age group—the "tutor" could even be mom or dad.

Of course it's not always possible to tutor your own child, as much as you would like to. And perhaps you might be concerned that you don't have either the patience or the skills to take on the challenge of bringing your child up to speed in reading. Or, in the midst of all your other responsibilities, there just might not be enough time to give the job the attention it deserves. Whatever the reason, a private tutor could be just what your child needs.

Tutors are especially effective for children who lack confidence in their reading abilities and who fear failure or the ridicule of their classmates. Children can be quite cruel about the shortcomings of their peers, and some first and second graders are particularly sensitive to this form of public scrutiny. For these children it is especially difficult to appreciate the wisdom that learning or succeeding at anything involves a chain of failures. Working with a tutor, however, allows a child to take her reading tumbles in private, knowing that she'll be helped up and dusted off after every fall. With a tutor's encouragement, a child's reading skills and personal confidence can grow in a safe haven. Even a basic one-session-a-week tutoring schedule during the summer can help young students maintain their hard-won skills.

WHAT TO EXPECT FROM YOUR CHILD'S TUTOR

A private tutor should be able to work with your child at his own pace, and use whatever materials and methods it takes to encourage him to read. The tutor should be flexible about teaching strategies and learning aids, and should quickly develop a feel for your child's aptitudes and preferences. Some tutors prefer to use a particular set of worksheets or series of books when they are working with a child who has a specific, definable academic need. For example, phonics-based worksheets might be exactly what your child needs to help develop his reading skills. A rigid approach to tutoring, on the other hand, is counterproductive. So even a tutor who usually relies on worksheets or a particular series of books, should be flexible about using alternative materials, such as flash cards with a child who learns visually, colorful letter blocks for a tactile learner, or tapes for a child who is an auditory learner.

Most importantly, a tutor's plan should be structured to give your child success. Optimally, your child should emerge from her tutoring session saying, "I did it!" Even a very small achievement is an amazing motivator. Each success is a stepping-stone to another. The goal of your child's tutor, therefore, should be to give her at least one small victory in every hour they're together. You'll want to be certain that your child's tutor is as dedicated to this concept as you are—and in all likelihood she will be.

THE NUTS AND BOLTS OF HIRING A TUTOR

Most tutoring arrangements work the way a regular music lesson might:

➤ Each session lasts an hour, and it falls on the same day each week at a regular time. Don't hesitate to ask a

prospective tutor about more flexible arrangements—
many work very hard to accommodate special situations
and schedules.

➤ Some tutors teach in their own homes. Others are willing
to come to your child and work with her in your own
home. Be aware that most tutors work with several children at a time, all of whose lessons must fit neatly into a
limited number of after-school hours in any given week.
A departure from this schedule might be hard to arrange
at times—or it might cost you a little extra. Tutoring costs
can vary a great deal, depending on where you live, as
well as your child's grade level. Generally, the lower the
grade level, the lower the cost of a tutor.

➤ An experienced, certified classroom teacher would expect
about $25 to $35 per hour for tutoring a first or second
grader. (If your child has a diagnosed learning disability,
her needs—and tutoring costs—may be greater.)

➤ Teachers in graduate programs, or undergraduates who
are considering a teaching career, are also excellent candidates. These soon-to-be professionals are often eager to
gain teaching experience and generally charge less than
seasoned tutors.

➤ A student teacher should be able to give your child the
practice, structure, and one-on-one support she needs.
Give this tutoring option a shot, especially if budget is a
factor and you live in or near a college town.

➤ College students make wonderful tutors, especially in the
lower grades—and usually charge less than professional
tutors.

EXPLORING THE OPTIONS:
HOW TO FIND A TUTOR

Finding the right tutor for your child can be tricky. For one thing,
you want to find someone you can trust to be alone with your
child on a regular basis. So, for safety's sake, it's crucial to get recommendations from people you know, or from parents who have
retained the tutor's services. At the same time, the tutor you hire
has to be someone your child can trust and who will be supportive yet challenging, all through the learning process.

It may take a while to find the right tutor for your child but
don't give up. Quality one-on-one attention from a committed and

trustworthy adult is the best thing you can give your child if he needs help with reading. Few other skills will be more important to him as he progresses from grade to grade. Finding a good tutor needn't be a source of anxiety if you think of the experience as a positive one for your whole family. In the end, all of you will benefit from your child's newfound confidence and delight in reading.

Schoolteachers

Although many classroom teachers tutor after school or on weekends, it is generally understood that a child's own classroom teacher is off limits because the potential for a conflict of interest is too great. At the very least, an exchange of money between a student's parent and a classroom teacher *looks* suspicious to the parents of other children in the class. Even though your child's classroom teacher is out of the running as a tutor, he may very well be able to recommend tutors to you, especially if he has a good understanding of your child's educational needs. If this is the case, he will probably know of a tutor who will mesh well with your child.

Alternatively, a teacher in the school, a teaching assistant, or teacher's aide can be a terrific choice. Your child may already be familiar with school staffers, just from seeing them on lunch duty or in the halls, and their association with the school can be a powerful motivator for your child. (If you've ever noticed a kid suddenly switch into best-behavior mode when she runs into a teacher from her school in the supermarket or at a park, you've seen this effect in action. For many children, anyone associated with the authority structure of school carries a whiff of that same authority. A close association between tutor and school can help keep such kids on track.) It can be enormously beneficial for your child to be tutored by a teacher at his school because she has access to your child's homeroom teacher as well as other staff who have regular contact with him. Therefore, she can find out specific information about your child's reading difficulties and zero in on them. In addition, teachers from your child's school will be intimately familiar with the reading program in use there. They'll know both how it functions and which learning concepts will be coming up next for your child. This is a huge advantage because it gives the teacher/tutor the ability to anticipate and smooth the academic path for your child with particular exercises and preparatory work.

The School Principal

If your child's classroom teacher can't give you any leads, try asking the principal's office for recommendations. Many principals maintain lists of qualified teachers who are looking for tutoring work. Generally, an administrator's pool of contacts is broader than that of any one classroom teacher, and it encompasses teachers at every grade level, including substitute and retired teachers, and teachers on leave. Therefore, your chances of finding a good match through the principal's office might be better than going through an individual teacher.

Friends and Neighbors

Another good source for tips about tutors is conveniently close to home—your friends and neighbors. Ask family members, other parents in your child's class, people in the block association—or just about any acquaintance you can think of—if he or she knows of a good tutor. You may be surprised by the number of people in your community who are either active or retired teachers. As one mother observed, "Your neighbor is probably a teacher, but if she isn't, her sister is." Retired teachers, full- or part-time substitute teachers, and teachers on parental (or other) leave from school will frequently take on tutoring work, as will some full-time instructors.

On the other hand, some children are more comfortable using a tutor outside the school loop, or working with someone they already know as a family friend. This kind of relationship can make up for whatever networking benefits a tutor who is connected to your child's school might bring to the job. But unless you know the person well, don't be shy about asking for references, and following up on them.

Colleges

Some colleges offer assessment and tutoring programs for the benefit of children who live nearby. And for many parents the education department at the local college is right at the top of their list for tutoring services.

Student tutors are enthusiastic and motivated, and usually charge less than experienced teachers do. And since tutoring programs are part of the education department, student tutors (and your child) have the benefit of their professors' experience if they encounter teaching problems or difficulties. But again, references are key. Be sure to contact former employers before hiring a tutor.

Broadening Your Network: The Internet and Other Sources of Information

If your own network of contacts can't help you locate the right tutor for your child, there are plenty of commercial organizations that can. Check your local phone directory under "Tutorial Services" and you're more than likely to find referral services or private tutors. The perfect match for your child could be found there. Or try the Internet. Several websites serve as tutor clearinghouses that collect data about various kinds of private tutors who work in your area. For example, Tutor.com (www.tutor.com) is a directory and matching service that you can search by zip code and sort by hourly cost, certification level, or distance from your home. It includes more than 8,000 tutors nationwide.

Another service, 1-800-TUTORS (www.1800tutors.com) lists tutors by state and specialty and gives you a paragraph-long profile of the tutor, which may or may not include his or her going rate. Keep in mind that tutor clearinghouses do not check the background or certification of the instructors they list. Generally, people pay to be listed on a website as a tutor, and they create their own listings. Therefore, be sure to check references before you hiring anyone.

Tutoring Centers and Franchise Learning Centers

In many areas, the demand for tutoring help has become so great that both independent tutoring centers and franchise learning centers are thriving. Independent centers are frequently owned and staffed by current or former state-certified teachers, and vary widely in atmosphere and teaching techniques. Franchise centers generally adhere to certain centrally controlled standards that apply to both curriculum and décor. Either of these types of learning center may offer one-on-one learning, but a revolving staff makes it less likely for them to provide your child with the consistency that a traditional tutoring relationship fosters. Before choosing a center be sure to visit it on your own and then with your child to get a good sense of how it operates and whether your child will feel comfortable there.

HOW TO EVALUATE A POTENTIAL TUTOR

Once you've gathered a good list of recommended tutors, make telephone contacts with each tutor on you list. If you are not sure of what to ask, try the following questions:

➤ How long have you been working with children?

➤ What grade levels have you taught?

➤ Are you a certified teacher?

➤ What is your own educational background?

➤ How many years of tutoring experience do you have?

➤ How long do your tutoring relationships typically last?

➤ Would my child be working with you one-on-one or in a group?

➤ Where do you prefer to work?

➤ Do you have any experience teaching children with special needs or learning disabilities?

➤ How would you evaluate my child's learning needs?

➤ Will you develop a learning plan for my child?

➤ How would you evaluate my child's ongoing progress?

➤ How would you work with my child's classroom teacher?

➤ Please give me a step-by-step description of one of your tutoring sessions.

➤ What books and materials do you use in tutoring sessions? May I review them?

➤ Will you work with my child on her regular homework?

➤ May I have several references? Both colleagues and parents of children you've tutored would be helpful.

➤ Please tell me about your schedule and your fees.

When these and other questions have been answered to your satisfaction, check references and follow up with past clients—for your child's safety and your own peace of mind. Call the tutor and arrange to meet. Having a face-to-face impression of the potential tutor will be an important factor in the hiring process.

Perhaps the most important reason to meet a potential tutor face-to-face is to get a sense of the *person* who will be spending so much time with your child. After all, you want to be as certain as you can be that he is both capable of reaching your child and treating her with every consideration. Here are some suggestions:

➤ Set up a "get-acquainted" session with the prospective tutor and your child. Meeting for an informal lunch or an afternoon ice cream cone is a pleasant way to break the ice.

➤ Listen carefully to what your child thinks and feels about the tutor.

➤ If the tutor's comments about what she wants to focus on with your child meet with your approval—and of course if your child likes and feels comfortable with her—you've found the right tutor.

Once you know the facts about price, schedule, and location, you will want to know more about how the tutor will deal with certain situations that may arise during their sessions. Below are some questions you may want to ask to better understand how your child's tutor will handle more difficult situations.

Sample Situations

1. If you spend three weeks working through the same decoding problem and my child still doesn't understand the concept, do you let him give up so that he doesn't face failure?

2. What is more important, your success as a tutor, or my child's success at reading?

3. If my child says to you that he is ready to give up, how would you encourage him to stick with it and not become discouraged?

4. If my child does well at each session, but is unable to retain what he has learned from week to week, what will you do to help him remember what he is learning?

5. How do you motivate/reward my child while maintaining the importance of what is learned, not what the next reward will be?

Ask *even more* questions to determine whether a potential tutor will be able to build a good rapport with your child. As we've said before, you know your child best!

Sample "Rapport" Questions

1. My child is very shy, how will you try to establish a relationship with him?

2. How will you maintain a friendship with my child, while still representing yourself as an authority figure?

3. If my child is having discipline problems during sessions, how will you deal with the situation?

A GOOD LEARNING ENVIRONMENT

Like the "homework zone" mentioned in Chapter 6, a good learning environment should be a clean, well-lighted space free of distractions. If your child is going to be tutored outside of your home, you certainly will want to see the environment in which your child will be working. There should be educational elements, such as a poster of the alphabet, a chalkboard, or other educational materials such as alphabet flashcards or magnetic letters, so that a child is stimulated to learn. The child should have a comfortable place to sit and a desk that is the right size for him. And, don't hesitate to ask a prospective tutor about implementing more flexible arrangements—many work very hard to accommodate special needs.

> **"**A relaxed, trusting and productive relationship between tutor and child is important to maintain. If a child doesn't want to be tutored, if she doesn't feel that she's really cared about, and if the tutor is not enthusiastic about working with her, the child is not going to absorb what she needs to learn no matter how "good" the teacher is.**"**
>
> —A MOM FROM NEW YORK

HOW TO WORK WITH YOUR CHILD'S TUTOR

If the tutoring relationship works well, it can be a powerful force for change in your child's life, academically, emotionally, and even socially. Give your child and her tutor some space and breathing room. Feel free to come in every once in a while to make sure everything's all right, but let your child and the tutor work. It's important for you to cultivate your child's relationship with his tutor. They have to trust each other to do their work, and that takes some time. Encourage them to use a few minutes of their hour to play a game, have some fun, and laugh. After all, if your child isn't having *some* fun, it will be difficult for him to enjoy the experience.

Be sure to talk to your child after each tutoring session. Draw her out; ask her to tell you what she did *right* that day. Focus on that accomplishment, praise her for it, and encourage her to remember the lesson as a successful one. Don't dwell on any of the negative things she may have said about the lesson. (Do remember them however, and bring them up with the tutor if they raise concerns for you.) Keep in mind that a child's recollection of an experience, even a very recent one, can be skewed by his feelings in the last ten minutes. So try to pick up on body language and facial expression to get a sense of your child's take on how things are really going.

TUTOR CHECKLIST

As you search for the right tutor for your child, use this checklist to make sure you've asked all the right questions and covered all the bases. Remember, you're looking to create a relationship on your child's behalf. Trust your instincts.

- ❏ Ask classroom teacher for recommendations.
- ❏ Ask school administrators for recommendations.
- ❏ Ask friends and neighbors for recommendations.
- ❏ Check phone book and websites.
- ❏ Use phone interviews and ask all relevant questions to narrow list of tutors.
- ❏ Ask for references—past clients you can talk to.
- ❏ Call references to check on tutors past performance, trustworthiness, and demeanor.
- ❏ Meet tutor where lessons would take place—tutor's home, classroom or learning center, or your home.
- ❏ Look at tutor's suggested teaching materials: are they appropriate for your child?
- ❏ Try to imagine your child working with this person. Will their personalities mesh or clash?
- ❏ Have child meet tutor where lessons would take place.
- ❏ Observe them interact in a simple word game or flash card drill.
- ❏ Ask your child for any reactions.
- ❏ Work with tutor to devise a regular lesson schedule.

Be sure to ask how the tutor deals with special projects and long-term home-work assignments. Many tutors are willing to use lesson time or set up a special meeting to help a child work on a challenging book report or other project. If you think your child will need adult assistance with these kinds of assignments, find out in advance if the tutor is willing to pitch in.

It is also important for you to communicate with the tutor on a regular basis. If possible, speak privately, out of your child's hearing, so that you can speak honestly without worrying your child or hurting his feelings. Emphasize the positive changes you're seeing. Then ask questions, and describe your concerns about problem areas. Between tutoring sessions keep a running list of the skills and concepts that continue to give your child trouble. Also note the homework assignments he gets stuck on, the words he has problems decoding, and so on. Share your observations with the tutor at the beginning of each session—or better yet, a day or so beforehand. Keeping her informed would be a great help to her in addressing the issues that are most relevant to your child at every session.

If the tutor you've hired is not connected to your child's school, do what you can to help the tutor and the classroom teacher connect. As professionals, they will want and need to share assessments and teaching strategies. Speak to the classroom teacher or write a note to her first: "My child is working with a new tutor, and they seem to be working well together. I think it would be helpful if the tutor could speak with you to resolve some questions and understand the classroom routine. Would it be possible for the tutor to call and speak with you sometime soon? Please let me know when and how she might get in contact with you." In this relationship, however, remember that you have to be the intermediary. Talking to the classroom teacher is not something that most tutors do as a matter of course. If you want it to happen, however, *you* have to be the one to make sure that it does. It's a great advantage for the tutor and the classroom teacher to talk to one another because it gives both of them useful insights into your child's learning strengths and weaknesses. If the tutor is working blindly, without the advantage of knowing what a child's learning problems are, it could take a few weeks or a month of one-on-one work with that child to finally focus on the most important issues. Even though your child is receiving tutorial help, she still needs you to read and play with her, and to encourage her progress. Her tutor should be willing and eager to assist you, in you're support-ing role, by passing along suggestions about what is working with your child in their tutoring sessions. There should always be time to talk with you about your child's progress and problems along the way.

Remember that tutors are people too. They need reassurance from you that their work is noticed and appreciated. If you're tak-ing regular notes on your child's reading struggles, don't forget to jot down whatever positive steps and new achievements you've seen in your child's work. Share these triumphs, large and small, with the tutor. Be sure to let him see your child's report cards, marked tests, and returned essays and assignments, too. He deserves to enjoy your child's success along with you.

Bringing a creative and caring tutor into your child's life could make all the difference in his school career. Even a weekly meet-ing over the summer months can significantly boost a child's con-fidence in his ability to read and enjoy words. It may sound like a tall order, but matching your child with the right tutor doesn't have to be an ordeal. However, it does take some time, thought, and planning.

This chapter has provided essential information about finding, hiring, paying for, and building a working relationship with your child's tutor. However, the importance of checking references and meeting in person before hiring a tutor cannot be over-empha-sized. In all likelihood your efforts will result in a happy and pro-ductive match between your child and a caring adult, but even when the tutor is on board don't forget that your child still needs *you* to encourage her progress and celebrate each new victory.

Resources

LEARNING CENTERS

Huntington Learning Centers   1-800-CAN-LEARN

Huntington Learning Centers have been operating for more than twenty years to provide tutoring and educational support to young students. Children are taught in small groups with a curriculum based on the results of an initial diagnostic placement test. Depending on the child's needs and weaknesses, her Huntington program may focus on reading, math, study habits, and so on. The chain prides itself on an ability to "break the failure chain" with an emphasis on basic skills instruction, motivational techniques, and an increase in the child's self-confidence. The Huntington website (www.huntingtonlearning.com) features an easy-to-use location finder, parent-to-parent advice, and helpful checklists.

Sylvan Learning Centers   1-888-EDUCATE

With nearly 800 locations across the country, Sylvan is one of the best-known education franchises in the country. Centers use a kind of positive-reinforcement technique, involving tokens that are redeemable in an on-site toy store, to motivate students. Students follow a personalized curriculum based on the results of the initial assessment tests taken by the child. Sylvan guarantees that its students' reading skills will improve by one full grade level after thirty-six hours of instruction—if not, the child will receive twelve additional hours of class time for free.

The company's national website, www.educate.com, includes a "discovery tool" that helps parents assess their child's strengths and weaknesses, as well as parenting tips, an education Q&A, a center finder, and information on the Sylvan learning philosophy.

SCORE! Educational Centers   1-888-ESCORE4

A new and growing arm of the Kaplan test-prep empire, SCORE! centers focus on supporting elementary, middle, and high schoolers. Outlets can be found throughout California, and in some parts of Colorado, Connecticut, Illinois, Maryland, Massachusetts, New Jersey, New York, and Virginia. The SCORE! program is adaptive, tailored to each student's skill level. Students work at a particular level of difficulty in their chosen program, and they move ahead when they are ready to, guided by "Academic Coaches." Following something of a health club model, membership in a local center entitles students to one or two weekly hourlong sessions, which can be made at their own convenience.

HOME PROGRAMS

Hooked On Phonics

If decoding skills are the crux of your child's reading problem, this well-known program might be the answer. Hooked On Phonics has successfully helped thousands of young children master their decoding difficulties with sets of interlinked audiotapes, flash cards, workbooks, story books, and games. The program is designed specifically for home-based, parent-led use. It includes a "Parent's Toolbox" that contains guidance, tips, and ideas on how to get the most out of the program, as well as motivational aids like stickers and posters. With materials for five successive reading levels included in each package, Hooked On Phonics can support students from the pre-reading period all the way up through independent literacy.

The Hooked On Phonics Learn to Read Program comes in several variations, depending on the number of books included with the set, with prices ranging from $199.95 to $249.95. Orders can be placed and questions answered at 1-800-532-3607. The company's website, www.hop.com, includes guidance features for parents, including an assessment-test feature and a question-and-answer forum.

> **"**I've had parents use Hooked On Phonics, and it works. It covers the mechanics of decoding. But I wish more parents would carry the program to its next level, to comprehension. Most don't carry it that far . . . they don't realize that they can keep using it to build comprehension skills as well.**"**
>
> —First-grade teacher, Susan Todd

The Phonics Game

More of a learning system than a game, The Phonics Game aims to teach children the sounds of the English language—along with its forty-three spelling rules—through a series of six progressive card games, supported by video and audiotapes, charts, storybooks, and other resources. The games spur players to say the various letter sounds as they hear them and see the letters that make them, leading to a quick and effective learning process. The associated storybooks are designed to work with the skills that the games have taught, giving young readers the sense of success that is so crucial to the learning process. Various versions of The Phonics Game are available, from a "Starter Kit" containing just three of the card games and a videotape to the "Total Learning System," which comes with all six games, several videos, audiotapes, storybooks, and more. Any version can be ordered by phone at 1-888-713-GAME, or online (www.phonicsgame.com) prices range from $79.99 to $284.85.

School Zone Workbook Series

Designed specifically for home use, School Zone workbooks teach readiness and basic skills. The company's book series are meant to work in harmony to supplement the school curriculum. Bright illustrations and clear instructions make them ideal for first and second graders. School Zone also produces tie-in flash card sets and CD-ROMs. The products are available in many school-supply and teacher stores, or you can order online (www.school-zone.com). The website offers special samplers of materials (books, cards, and workbooks emphasizing reading and math skills) for the first- and second-grade levels.

INTERNET LEARNING

Electronic Bus   www.e-bus.com

The Nechako Electronic Busing Program is a service of the Ministry of Education of British Columbia, Canada, which is responsible for a large number of home-schooled students. The program essentially provides the British Columbia public schools' curriculum to students from kindergarten through high school in any setting they wish, via the Internet and e-mail. The Electronic Bus site includes some terrific word games, tips for encouraging young readers and writers, and themed Internet links.

The Learning Odyssey   www.childu.com

A complete home learning curriculum for elementary and middle-school students (kindergarten through eighth grade), The Learning Odyssey can be adapted for your child's needs—from homeschooling to enrichment of a traditional school program. After taking a free online placement test, the student is set up with an individualized curriculum in any (or every) subject area, from reading to science to history. Students work at their own pace, moving on to new levels as previous ones are mastered. Staff teachers can be reached at any time by e-mail or by telephone, but the system is designed so that a student's records can be closely monitored by a parent, tutor, or teacher.

INTERNET PARENTING MATERIALS

Childfun.com   www.childfun.com

This site includes a column called "Ask the Teacher" that addresses such weekly topics as how to find a tutor. You'll also find great ideas for activities, crafts, and other fun things that kids and parents can do together.

Parentsoup.com   www.parentsoup.com

The main attraction of the Parentsoup site is its excellent collection of themed newsgroups, which let parents network their way through problems with the help of other parents and the occasional expert.

Rightstart.com   www.rightstart.com

At heart an on-line catalog of children's gear (see "Stores" for more), The Right Start's site also offers useful Q & A-style columns, including "Ask the Librarian" and "Ask the Teacher," that accept parents' questions for use in their online features.

PARENTING MAGAZINES

Family Life Magazine

Aimed at parents of children going through the "middle years"—ages five to twelve—*Family Life* runs features on child development, education, crafts, travel, food, and toys. Its mission is to help readers "embrace the unique challenges and joys of the busy years when your family is your life."

Mothering Magazine

With a focus on attachment parenting and "natural family living," this is the alternative press of parenting publications. *Mothering*, which publishes six issues a year, offers regular features on home-schooling and other educational methods, as well as columns on new children's books. Its website (www.mothering.com) offers subject-specific forums on various parenting topics, including education.

Offspring Magazine

One of the newest of the genre, *Offspring* caters to parents of school-age children. With a heavy focus on technology, you'll find reviews of the latest CD-ROMs, useful websites, and computer accessories, as well as more general features on parenting issues. *Offspring* is published every other month.

Parents Magazine

Parents is one of the best-known monthlies for moms and dads. You'll find a primary focus on the issues of babies, toddlers, and preschoolers, but *Parents* offers features on the needs of older children as well. The magazine's website, www.parents.com, contains a "Development" section with archived articles on education topics, among others, organized by age group.

Sesame Street Parents

Aimed at parents of preschoolers through primary graders, this monthly magazine features a regular column on how parents can support the learning process for their five to eleven year olds. Subscribers get the magazine for free when they order the children's monthly *Sesame Street*, not a bad deal if your household includes younger children as well. (Or you can check out the features online at www.sesamestreet.org.)

BOOKS ON PARENTING

What Your First Grader Needs to Know: Fundamentals of a Good First Grade Education, by E. D. Hirsch, Editor (Dell, 1998) and *What Your Second Grader Needs to Know: Fundamentals of a Good Second-Grade Education*, by E. D. Hirsch and John Holdren, Editors (Doubleday, 1998). Part of the Core Knowledge book series, these two volumes advocate the "knowledge-based curriculum" for first and second graders. The editor, who is the author of the best-selling book *Cultural Literacy*, believes that both children and adults need to master a fundamental set of facts in order to progress in school and in society. These books break Hirsch's ideas down grade by grade, and provide exercises and read-aloud stories that parents can use to help teach the core knowledge elements—including Greek mythology, American history, science, and math—to their children.

The Educated Child: A Parent's Guide from Preschool Through Eighth Grade, by William J. Bennett, et al. (Free Press, 1999). This massive tome outlines what to look for—and perhaps more importantly, avoid—in a grammar-school education for your children. William J. Bennett is a conservative writer, critic, and sometime political candidate. Author of *The Book of Virtues* and several other books, he and his co-authors call for a return to standards and the classics.

Teach Your Child to Read in 100 Easy Lessons, by Siegfried Engelmann, et al. (Simon & Schuster, 1986). There are parents who swear by this method, a home learning course in a book. The curriculum explained in *Teach Your Child to Read* can be easily supervised by any parent. It takes some commitment, though, and a willingness to follow the program lesson for lesson. Each session takes about twenty minutes to complete, taking children beyond letter recognition and basic phonics up through comprehension and real, independent reading.

Every Child Can Succeed: Making the Most of Your Child's Learning Style, by Cynthia Ulrich Tobias (Focus on the Family, 1999). The author says that you can't build on weaknesses, only on strengths—so if you can analyze your child's strengths, you can work with them to build up their self-confidence and potential for success. This book describes the various learning styles in depth and helps parents apply the concept to their own child's personality.

To Read or Not to Read, by Daphne M. Hurford (Simon & Schuster, 1999). This book focuses on dyslexia, a term that really covers any difficulty with the written word, whether the problem emerges in reading or in writing. *To Read or Not to Read* is a comprehensive and sensitive exploration of this widely misunderstood disorder.

STORES

Hammett's Learning World   www.hammett.com

With more than seventy stores across the country, Hammett's is the best-known teacher's resource in the nation. Many parents know the chain for its broad selection of art supplies and educational toys, but each store also carries a range of classroom books, decorations, learning aids, and other materials that are terrific for home use as well. And Hammett's selection of workbooks for every skill and grade level is unmatched. The company's website, www.hammett.com, includes a store locator feature, an online catalog, online shopping, message boards, chat rooms, lesson plans, and an excellent list of educational links.

The Teacher's Store   www.theteacherstore.com

This online resource is aimed especially toward classroom teachers and home-schooling parents, but any student could benefit from its well-chosen products. A wonderfully detailed table of contents points you toward materials that are sure to interest and motivate your child, from graphic organizers to reward badges. Featuring workbooks from Scholastic and Evan Moore, educational puzzles and toys, maps and charts, most materials are organized by age range and all are fully searchable. The store itself is based in Worcester, Massachusetts.

The Right Start   www.rightstart.com

This chain has franchises in sixteen states from coast to coast. Along with developmental toys for newborns through school-age children, clothing, books, and other child-related goodies, most stores contain a teachers' section with a nice array of flash cards, workbooks, wall charts, and supplies. The chain's website, www.rightstart.com, offers these materials as well.

GAMES

Reader Rabbit

The Reader Rabbit series of CD-ROM games is well-regarded by teachers and kids alike. It's known for putting educational games in the context of an interesting story line. For example, Reader Rabbit 1st Grade sets the player in an old theater in the hours before a variety show is to take the stage. The games are all part of the last-minute preparations, from money-counting to script-writing. The series is wide-ranging, so the games listed below are most likely to appeal to your first or second grader.

Reader Rabbit 2 (Ages 5–8)

Using the theme of a railroad journey, Reader Rabbit 2 develops players' phonics and reading skills, including word building, vowel-sound recognition, word concepts, and alphabetization. Featuring several levels of difficulty that challenge children to improve, the CD also uses technical flourishes such as lifelike digitized speech, which helps children associate letters and words with their corresponding sounds.

Reader Rabbit Reading (Ages 6–9)

This CD encourages reading and writing through imaginative thinking. With 100 reading lessons, forty interactive stories, and several phonics games, it keeps kids learning for hours. The CD even includes a feature that lets children record themselves reading their own stories.

Reader Rabbit 1st Grade and Reader Rabbit 2nd Grade

These CDs present a series of interrelated games—fourteen and ten of them, respectively—that focus on various grade-level skills, including phonics, science, math, and creativity. Each game has several skill levels, so play can become more challenging as the player masters the concept. The CDs include progress charts so students (and parents) can track their improving skills.

Reading Blaster

Another well-known educational series, the "Blaster" games are known for their arcade-like play and especially their excellent music and sound effects (take note, for auditory learners).

Reading Blaster 1st Grade

This series of games reinforce letter-sound recognition, identification of the parts of speech, writing, and reading. The games proceed through five levels of difficulty and feature 1,500 vocabulary words. Kids especially love the "Sticker Maker" feature.

Reading Blaster 2nd Grade

These games review the first-grade skills and then expand into working with contractions, compound words, syllables, prefixes, and suffixes. They also introduce 1,700 spelling words, as well as crosswords and word-search puzzles.

READING MATERIALS KIDS LOVE

Magazines

Disney Adventure
Highlights for Children
Ladybug
National Geographic World
Nickelodeon Magazine
Sports Illustrated for Kids
Turtle

Books for Emerging Readers

A You're Adorable, by Martha Alexander (Candlewick Press, 1998)
Caps for Sale, by Esphyr Slobodkina (HarperTrophy, 1987)
The Carrot Seed, by Ruth Krauss (HarperTrophy, 1989)
Harold and the Purple Crayon, by Crockett Johnson (HarperCollins, 1981)
In the Small, Small Pond, by Denise Fleming (Henry Holt, 1998)
Madeline series by Ludwig Bemelmans (Viking Press, 1993)
Make Way for Ducklings, by Robert McCloskey (Puffin Books, 1999)
Millions of Cats, by Wanda Gag (Paper Star, 1996)

The Napping House, by Audrey Wood (Red Wagon, 1996)

The Snowy Day, by Ezra Jack Keats (Viking Press, 1996)

Where the Wild Things Are, by Maurice Sendak (HarperCollins, 1988)

Books for First Graders

Alexander and the Terrible, Horrible, No Good, Very Bad Day, by Judith Viorst (Aladdin, 1987)

Amelia Bedelia, by Peggy Parish (HarperCollins, 1992)

Bread and Jam for Frances, by Russell Hoban (HarperTrophy, 1993)

Bunny Money, by Rosemary Wells (Dial, 1997)

Chicken Soup with Rice, by Maurice Sendak (Harper Trophy, 1991)

Corduroy, by Don Freeman (Viking, 1976)

Curious George series by H. A. Rey (Houghton Mifflin, 1973)

Frog and Toad Are Friends, by Arnold Lobel (HarperCollins, 1979)

Horton Hatches the Egg, by Dr. Seuss (Random House, 1966)

If You Give a Mouse a Cookie, by Laura J. Numeroff (HarperCollins, 1985)

Lilly's Purple Plastic Purse, by Kevin Henkes (Greenwillow, 1996)

Little Bear series by Else Holmelund Minarik (HarperTrophy, 1978)

Look-Alikes, by Joan Steiner (Little Brown, 1998)

No, David!, by David Shannon (Scholastic, 1998)

Officer Buckle and Gloria, by Peggy Rathman (Putnam, 1995)

Pete's A Pizza, by William Steig (HarperCollins, 1998)

Stellaluna, by Jannell Cannon (Voyager Picture Book, 1997)

Strega Nona, by Tomie de Paola (Aladdin, 1988)

The True Story of the Three Little Pigs, by A. Wolf, by Jon Scieszka (Penguin, 1991)

Two Bad Ants, by Chris Van Allsburg (Houghton Mifflin, 1998)

The Very Busy Spider, by Eric Carle (Philomel Books, 1995)

The Very Hungry Caterpillar, by Eric Carle (Putnam, 1984)

The Z was Zapped, by Chris Van Allsburg (Walter Lorraine, 1998)

Books for Second Graders

A to Z Mysteries, series by Ron Roy (Knopf)

Amber Brown Is Not a Crayon, by Paula Danziger (Scholastic, 1995)

Arthur series, by Marc Brown (Random House)

Captain Underpants series, by Dav Pilkey (Little Apple)
Cody's Secret Admirer, by Betsy Duffey (Viking, 1998)
Encyclopedia Brown series, by Donald J. Sobol (Bantam)
Henry and Mudge series by Cynthia Rylant (Aladdin)
Jumanji, by Chris Van Allsburg (Houghton Mifflin, 1981)
Junie B. Jones and Some Sneaky Peeky Spying, by Barbara Park (Random House, 1994)
Magic Tree House series, by Marion Pope Osborne (Random House)
Math Curse, by Jon Scieszka (Viking, 1995)
Nate the Great series, by Marjorie Weinman Sharmat (Yearling)
Pinky & Rex, by James Howe (Simon & Schuster, 1998)
The Polar Express, by Chris Van Allsburg (Houghton Mifflin, 1985)
See You Around, Sam, by Lois Lowry (Houghton Mifflin, 1996)
Willy the Dreamer, by Anthony Browne (Candlewick, 1998)

Read-With-Me Books

A Wrinkle in Time, by Madeleine L'Engle (Yearling Books, 1973)
Charlotte's Web, by E.B. White (HarperTrophy, 1999)
Half Magic, by Edward Eager (Harcourt Brace, 1999)
Harriet the Spy, by Louise Fitzhugh (HarperTrophy, 1996)
Harry Potter series, by J.K. Rowling (Arthur A. Levine Books, 1998)
James and the Giant Peach, by Roald Dahl (Knopf, 1996)
Just a Dream, by Chris Van Allsburg (Houghton Mifflin, 1990)
The Lion, the Witch, and the Wardrobe, by C.S. Lewis (HarperCollins, 1994)
The Magic School Bus series, by Joanna Cole (Scholastic Trade, 1990)
Ramona Quimby, Age 8, by Beverly Cleary (Camelot, 1992)
The Secret Garden, by Frances Hodgson Burnett (Bantam, 1987)
Wishbone series, by A. D. Francis (Lyrick Studios, 1998)
The Wretched Stone, by Chris Van Allsburg (Houghton Mifflin, 1991)

Keys To Your Child's Success

These LearningExpress parent's guides offer practical tips and tools for helping first, second and third graders get the most out of school life. Written by experts affiliated with Columbia University's Teacher's College (the world's eading graduate school of education), they cover the complete school experience-everything from subject-by-subject reviews of standard schoolwork to insights on participation in sports, art and music classes, and social activities.

All of these books include:

- Information on the major goals for today's grade school curriculum.

- Fun, instructional home activities that reinforce what is being learned at school

- Tips for helping children develop self-esteem and healthy social skills.

- Advice on fostering a positive parent-teacher relationship.